CHAINED
TO THE LAND

CHAINED TO THE LAND

Voices from Cotton & Cane Plantations

**FROM INTERVIEWS OF FORMER SLAVES
EDITED BY LYNETTE ATER TANNER**

John F. Blair, Publisher Winston-Salem, North Carolina

JOHN F. BLAIR,

PUBLISHER

1406 Plaza Drive
Winston-Salem, North Carolina 27103
www.blairpub.com

Library of Congress Cataloging-in-Publication Data

Chained to the land : voices from cotton & cane plantations : from interviews of former slaves / edited by Lynette Ater Tanner.
    pages   cm
  ISBN 978-0-89587-626-3 (alkaline paper) — ISBN 978-0-89587-628-7 (ebook)
1. Slaves—Louisiana—Interviews. 2. Freedmen—Louisiana—Interviews. 3. African Americans—Louisiana—Interviews. 4. Slaves—Louisiana—Social conditions—19th century—Sources. 5. Plantation life—Louisiana—History—19th century—Sources. 6. Slavery—Louisiana—History—19th century—Sources. 7. Louisiana—Race relations—History—19th century—Sources. 8. Louisiana—Biography. I. Tanner, Lynette Ater.
 E445.L8C47 2014
 306.3'620922—dc23
 [B]

        2014012556

10 9 8 7 6 5 4 3 2 1

DESIGN BY DEBRA LONG HAMPTON
COVER:
RED VINTAGE TEXTURE © DAVID M. SHRADER/SHUTTERSTOCK
OLD FABRIC TEXTURE © PHOTOCELL/SHUTTERSTOCK

Cover image: Percy Jefferson, whose family has lived on Frogmore Plantation for generations, is pictured in this photograph. He is a reenactor for historical tours and operates a modern cotton gin on the plantation.

CONTENTS

Preface ix
Acknowledgments xiii
Introduction: Louisiana, the Melting Pot xv

CONCORDIA PARISH/NATCHEZ AREA

Mary Reynolds 3
Silas Spotfore 14
Victoria Williams 18

WEST CARROLL PARISH

Edward Ashley 23

MONROE AREA

Mary Island 29
Mandy Johnson 31

Annie Parks 34
Charley Williams 40

BIENVILLE PARISH

Isaac Adams 59
Marion Johnson 65

ALEXANDRIA/CENTRAL LOUISIANA

Adam Hall 73
Isabella Jackson 77
Mandy Rollins 81

LAFAYETTE/OPELOUSAS AREA

Octavia Fontenette 87
Mary Ann John 90
Henry Reed 93
Carlyle Stewart 96

BATON ROUGE AREA

Catherine Cornelius 101
John McDonald 107
Albert Patterson 109
Robert St. Ann 114
Shack Wilson 120

NEW ORLEANS AREA

Peter Barber	129
Ellen Broomfield	138
Henrietta Butler	141
Manda Cooper	143
Martin Dragney	146
Mrs. M. S. Fayman	150
Rebecca Fletcher	155
Annie Flowers	163
Ceceil George	166
Mary Harris	173
Elizabeth Ross Hite	177
Odel Jackson	199
Daffney Johnson	202
Hannah Kelly	204
Frances Lewis	207
Hunton Love	215
Charles Pancanses	219
Gracie Stafford	221
Mrs. Webb	225
Julia Woodrich	227

PREFACE

Thankfully, over twenty-two hundred former slaves were interviewed in the 1930s as part of the Federal Writers' Project. John A. Lomax, the national advisor on folklore and folkways for the project, prepared a questionnaire that was issued April 22, 1937, as a supplement to *The American Guide Manual* for field workers. Most of the interviews were conducted in 1937–38. The project concluded in 1939–40.

The Federal Writers' Project, a division of the Works Progress Administration, issued guidelines for transcriptions. The interviewers were to avoid writing unintelligible pronunciations and were to make notations in parentheses. Barred spellings were listed: *Ah* for *I*; *baid* for *bed*; *cot* for *caught*; *cose* for *because*; *daid* for *dead*; *fiuh* or *fiah* for *fire*; *fuh* for *for*; *gi'* for *give*; *gwainter* for *going to*; *hit* for *it*; *ifn* for *if*; *j'in* for *join*; *kin'* for *kind*; *mah* for *my*; *moster* for *master*; *uthuh* for *other*; *ouh* for *our*; *ovah* for *over*; *poar* for *poor*; *tuh* for *to*; *undah* for *under*; *uz*, *uv*, or *o'* for *of*; *wuz* for *was*; *wha* or *whar* for *where*; *tho't* for *thought*; *oman* for *woman*; and *yo'* for *you*.

As is apparent in the narrations, most of the Louisiana interviewers used their own transcriptions for dialect.

Errors in grammar and punctuation are common since the former slaves spoke unpredictably, changing topics without notice. Run-on sentences are frequent; some sentences end with commas; some periods are used as commas. Additionally, the interviewers' grammatical skills were diverse. Some added vivid descriptions of the interviewees or their surroundings, while others added personal comments. Except where it affected clarity or readability, I have honored the integrity of these historical dialects and writing styles, complete with their many inconsistencies, in order to allow readers a glimpse into the times and the interviewees' lives. Insertions by the interviewers and occasionally by the ex-slaves themselves are in parentheses. My own editorial insertions are in brackets.

The project in Louisiana was spearheaded by Lyle Saxon of Natchitoches, who directed both the Louisiana Writers' Project and the Historical Records Survey until March 1937. Saxon was field supervisor of projects in Arkansas, Alabama, Florida, Georgia, Mississippi, North Carolina, South Carolina, Tennessee, and Louisiana and was director of Region VI, with responsibility for projects in Mississippi, Arkansas, Texas, and Oklahoma.

Most of the former slave narrations in this volume were kept in Natchitoches at Melrose Plantation, owned by Cammie Henry, a benefactor of the arts. That collection was subsequently donated to the Northwestern State University Archives in Natchitoches. DaNean Olene Pound deserves credit for analyzing and transcribing the difficult-to-read typewritten carbons and handwritten notes for her thesis when acquiring a master of arts in English.

In addition to the narratives housed in Louisiana, I have included those of slaves who lived and worked in Louisiana but resided in other states at the time of their interviews. Those narrations are housed in the Manuscript Division of the Library of Congress in Washington, D.C.

I have noted the ages of the former slaves at the time of the interviews when available and have chosen to include narrations that reflect a knowledge of slavery, the Civil War years, and the postwar years. Freedom brought hope of re-united families, an end to abuse, and compensated labor for the former slaves; however, for most freedmen, educational, financial, and political limitations soon squashed that hope.

Cotton and cane had powered the economy of Louisiana for 150 years, leaving few employment opportunities. The hoes and plows continued to be driven by those same hands, and once again they were bound. Occasionally, freedmen became landowners themselves, but most were resigned to dependence on former landowners. Years later, those aging sharecroppers had spent their entire lives on the land but could no longer work daylight to dark. Soon, the land was worked by the younger generation. Retirement to the cities brought with it insufficient incomes and local markets instead of garden plots, which spurred nostalgia for plantation days.

Abuse rampaged through Mary Reynolds's thoughts when she stated, "I members now clear as yesterday things I forgot for a long time." Conversely, Annie Flowers reminisced, "We jest sats down some times and talks about how we use to cut dat cane in them fields. . . . I knows it was happier times than now." Isaac Adams simply said, "Yes,

Lord, my old feets have been in mighty nigh every parish in Louisiana, and I seen some mighty pretty places, but I'll never forget how that old Gee plantation looked when I was a boy." Freeing themselves physically and then financially from the cotton and cane, these resilient former slaves were often still emotionally "chained to the land."

Many of the aged narrators were in their eighties, but some were over one hundred. Their recollections of food, housing, clothing, weddings, funerals, treatment, and relationships reflect an era like no other, for which America is still experiencing repercussions today. The interviewees' voices resonate with pride and anger, joy and sadness, and wit and wisdom. Through their eyes, I invite you to experience their Louisiana.

ACKNOWLEDGMENTS

For the past fifteen years at Frogmore Plantation, my staff and I have researched and interpreted slave narrations in order to share stories with visitors from around the globe. I thank Melissa Powell for her attention to detail and accuracy and Bethani Goodman for her enthusiasm in relating those narrations through word and song. With pride, the descendants of former Natchez District slaves have assisted with historical reenactments at Frogmore that relate the trials and triumphs of their ancestors: thank you to Dorothy Smith, Percy Jefferson, Margaret Leonard, Willie Minor, Edrena Lyons, and Beatrice Hunter.

Our historical tours center around twenty restored antebellum buildings. I am thankful for the constant maintenance provided by Charles Jefferson, Donald Jefferson, Randy Ainsworth, Chris Gannon, Gary Simpson, Alan Lanier, May Punchard, and Tommy Punchard. A special thank-you goes to Gloria Buckles for her assistance in every phase from reservations to preservation.

I thank my family for their encouragement and support. Finally, but most importantly, I thank my mother and our

Lord for instilling in me the desire to make a difference in generations to come by sharing these narrations, which not only detail mistakes of the past, but also reveal the importance of compassion, fairness, and Christian values for the future.

I dedicate this book to LaVonne Chapman Ater, my mother.

INTRODUCTION
LOUISIANA, THE MELTING POT

Louisiana, the vast land spanning from the Gulf of Mexico to New France (Canada) and west from the Appalachians to the tip of the Rockies, derived its name—La Louisiane, meaning "Land of Louis" (XIV)—from a French explorer, René-Robert Cavalier de La Salle, born in Rouen, France, in 1643. However, it was two brothers, Pierre Le Moyne d'Iberville and Jean-Baptiste Le Moyne de Bienville, who established the French settlements in southern Louisiana at Fort Maurepas and Fort Louis de la Mobile and who signed peace treaties with the Chickasaw and Choctaw tribes to establish fur trading. Iberville returned to France for supplies but died while there. In 1706, Bienville was appointed governor by the French government. By 1708, there were approximately three hundred settlers, most of whom were French soldiers; about twenty were women, as females did not want to leave France for such a wilderness, and many were Native American slaves. Provisions for the settlers were shipped from Europe and were scarce; farming was uncommon until later.

Finding the venture unprofitable, the French government

turned colonization of Louisiana over to two private French companies and appointed Antoine de La Mothe Sieur de Cadillac as governor. He arrived at Dauphin Island on Mobile Bay on June 5, 1713. Cadillac wrote in his notes of his disappointment in the natural resources of the land and the character of the settlers, calling them a "cut-throat set with no respect for religion."

Louis Juchereau de St. Denis, a cousin of Bienville, was sent on an expedition up the Red River and founded the French post of Natchitoches in 1714. However, Bienville and Cadillac disagreed on expenditures. Instead of using funds to set up more trading posts, Cadillac undertook a personal quest for gold. He caused further dissension when he ordered Bienville to Natchez with forty soldiers to stop the Indian attacks against French traders in the area. While there, Bienville supervised the construction of Fort Rosalie in 1716, but the colony continued to struggle. (See map on page xvii.)

When Bienville returned to Mobile, he was reappointed governor for his efforts toward peaceful Indian relations. During his tenure, Louisiana began to develop. Financier John Law received permission to organize the Company of the West, later known as the Mississippi Company, which controlled fur trading and mining in Louisiana. Law falsely advertised for colonists and gained seven thousand newcomers from Germany, Switzerland, and France, of whom twenty-five hundred were released prisoners arriving as indentured servants. In 1718, Bienville took some of the settlers to establish New Orleans, choosing a strategic site at a bend in the Mississippi near Lake Pontchartrain in order to

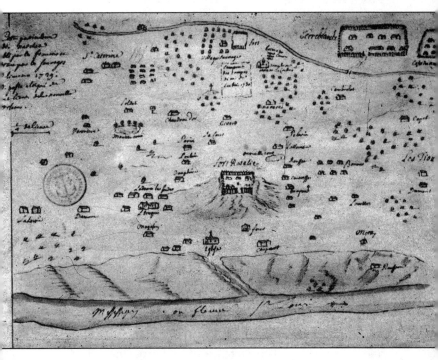

Map of Fort Rosalie

Courtesy of Natchez Historical Society

control goods shipped down the river. He also successfully transplanted sugarcane from the island of Martinique to his garden in New Orleans. These farmers emigrating from Germany and Switzerland were able to grow vegetables and raise cattle to help feed the French fur traders.

After Baton Rouge was established in 1719, Bienville received permission to move the capital from Mobile to New Orleans in 1722 to better safeguard trade on the river. By then, settlers in New Orleans had built cypress log cabins, a hospital, and a church for the Capuchin priests arriving to Christianize the Indians. The priests established the first boys' school on St. Ann Street in 1725. By 1727, nuns began the first girls' school in the United States, Ursuline Academy, which still operates today.

By the 1720s, the French in Louisiana had purchased six thousand slaves from Senegambia, West Africa (today's Senegal, Gambia, and Mali). French slave traders at their trading posts in West Africa purchased farmers accustomed to growing rice, corn, cotton, indigo, yams, peas, and greens. Some Africans were blacksmiths, weavers, and skilled artisans in making gold and silver jewelry. Most of the slave ships were unloaded at Fort Balize at the mouth of the Mississippi below New Orleans. Some slaves were sold in New Orleans and others shipped to Natchez or to far northern Louisiana (known as "the Illinois country") to assist in producing wheat, corn, and furs to be shipped downriver. The shipments to New Orleans from the Illinois country, in French boats called bateaux, took three or four weeks depending on the river's current; shipments upriver could take three to four months until steam power speeded the process in the 1800s.

French settlements in the Illinois territory were established at Kaskaskia, Cahokia, Fort de Chartres, St. Philippe, and Prairie du Rocher. Some slaves in transit were able to escape, taking food and ammunition to hunt and fish in the swamps. These runaways became known as "maroons."

Slavery in the 1720s spurred Louisiana crop production, including that of rice, tobacco, and indigo. Some slaves shadowed European craftsmen and acquired the skills of locksmiths, carpenters, blacksmiths, and shippers. The Natchez District had approximately 430 settlers and 1,900 slaves. However, fewer than 10 settlers owned 900 slaves, and 50 owned the other 1,000. The remaining 370 non-slave-owners existed as small farmers, traders, or artisans.

Le Code Noir, translated as "the Black Code," was enacted by the French in 1724 to set standards for clothing, food, and punishments for slaves; for converting slaves to Christianity; and for stipulating care for aging or ill slaves. This law was patterned after Le Code Noir as passed in France in 1685 to govern French Caribbean slaves. A similar law passed in 1792 during the Spanish reign allowed blacks and whites to marry and slaves more power to purchase their own freedom. The code was then adopted by the English with modifications and remained in effect until 1865, when the Thirteenth Amendment to the Constitution granted freedom to all slaves in the United States.

Slave life in Louisiana centered on families. Even though masters gave the slaves names, many retained their African names. Le Code Noir protected children from being sold from their parents until age fourteen; extended families were important. French masters could allow their

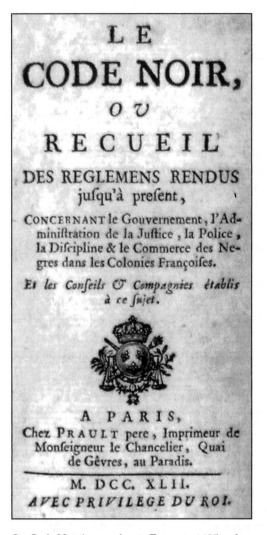

Le Code Noir became law in France in 1685 and was made legal in Louisiana in 1724.

slaves the right to grow and sell some of their vegetables and keep some of the money earned as artisans in order to eventually purchase their own freedom. Free blacks were able to purchase others in their families. Children born on American soil to Europeans or to intermarriages among Africans, Indians, and Europeans became known as Creoles, differentiating them from their foreign parents.

During Bienville's governorship from 1732 to 1743, Louisiana grew to sixty-four hundred settlers, of whom seventeen hundred were white and forty-seven hundred black. New Orleans records list eight hundred whites and three thousand blacks. Settlers and their slaves along the Mississippi from New Orleans to Illinois claimed long, narrow strips of land, built log cabins close to the water's edge, and used the river as their highway. Local officials called "Syndics" collected taxes and enforced laws.

Life in Louisiana was not without turmoil. The first slave revolt was planned in 1731 but was averted by French officials with the assistance of a slave woman in New Orleans. One of the leaders of the revolt was a slave named Samba, who was trusted by the officials of the Mississippi Company. Even though Le Code Noir mandated care and offered guidelines for slave disobedience, all plantation owners did not adhere to the law, and enforcement was difficult in remote areas. As in the Caribbean, revolts were triggered because of inhumane masters or overseers. French officials hired Louis Congo, a free man of color in New Orleans, as executioner for criminals; he served in that position for ten years in exchange for his family's freedom and a plot of land known as Congo Square, which later served as a Sunday gathering spot for slaves to participate in African dances and songs that helped preserve their culture. Today in New Orleans, that same plot houses the Mahalia Jackson Theater, which offers quality musicals and plays.

In contrast to New Orleans, turmoil in the early Natchez District stemmed more from Indian threats, especially after the French commander ordered the Indians at White Apple to vacate so French settlers could expand their tobacco fields. While some slaves assisted the Natchez Indians in hopes of gaining freedom, others assisted the French in exchange for that same promise. Half of the 430 settlers at Natchez died in the resulting battle, but those who survived nearly annihilated the Natchez Indians.

Turmoil continued with the onset of the French and Indian War against Britain (1754–63), which forever changed Louisiana. Before the war ended, France secretly ceded all of its lands west of the Mississippi to Spain in gratitude for Spain's assistance during the conflict. The British victory in 1763 forced France to cede all of its lands east of the Mississippi to Britain. (See map on page xxiii.) Simultaneously, the British governor in Acadie (now Nova Scotia) exiled all French citizens and ordered their homes burned. In hopes of finding French soil, many traveled to Louisiana, where they instead encountered Spanish rule and more tension. Their name, Acadians, was shortened to Cajuns.

Tensions eased temporarily when General Alejandro O'Reilly, the new Spanish authority, arrived. O'Reilly formed a *cabildo*, a council of Spanish and French men loyal to Spain. By 1795, the council began meeting in its new building, also named Cabildo; today, it still stands as a mu-

North America in 1700. French Louisiana extended from the Appalachians to the Rockies.

seum of Louisiana history. Shortly after the development of the *cabildo*, O'Reilly concentrated on establishing Fort Balize, a commercial port at the mouth of the Mississippi, and implemented a plan for the construction and maintenance of levees.

After the onset of the American Revolution and Britain's preoccupation with New England, the Spanish saw the opportunity to seize some of the British outposts that Spain had lost during the French and Indian War. Spain successfully regained control of Natchez, Mobile, and Pensacola from the British.

The slave population under Spanish rule increased to twenty-four thousand, and a unique culture not dictated by skin color developed in New Orleans. However, a lack of knowledge regarding sanitation and insect control caused high mortality rates among Europeans and slaves. The installation of street lighting exacerbated the insect problem; yellow fever and malaria epidemics were common. Hurricanes and fires—especially in 1788 and 1794—destroyed the cypress buildings. A Spanish residential contractor, Don Almonester, used over a hundred slaves to rebuild the city.

During that same era, Frenchman Jean Étienne de Boré hired a sugar maker from Saint-Domingue. Together, they introduced the sugar crystallization process to Louisiana in the 1790s, which was also when Eli Whitney was inventing the cotton gin in Georgia. Cotton gins were in the Natchez District by 1795. Expanding cotton and sugar production consumed more acres, thus demanding more slaves. East Coast slave owners plagued with infertile fields sold slaves to planters of the Mississippi Delta, whose fields were replenished by river silt deposited from the floods.

Louisiana once again became French in 1800, when Napoleon persuaded Spain to trade ownership of Louisiana land west of the Mississippi in exchange for European territory. Thomas Jefferson became concerned that Napoleon would shut down foreign trade in New Orleans, which was necessary to all the American colonies. With the intent of buying only New Orleans, Robert Livingston and Jefferson negotiated with French officials and ultimately purchased eight hundred thousand acres for $15 million.

Fifteen states from the Appalachians to the Rockies were once part of Louisiana. The state received its present boundaries in 1812, becoming the first state west of the Mississippi. To this day, it has kept its diverse culture.

Slavery continued in Louisiana until 1865. Before and since, African-Americans have contributed not only to plantations, households, restaurants, retail stores, hospitals, and ports, but also to the birth of blues, ragtime, jazz, zydeco, and the unique Louisiana cuisine that we call soul food and Cajun cooking. What flavor they have added to this melting pot of culture!

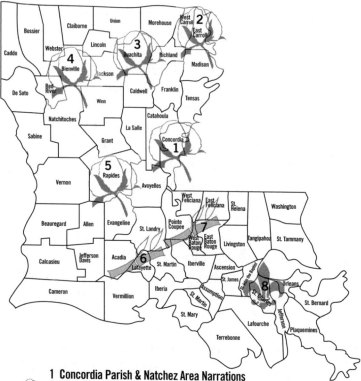

1 **Concordia Parish & Natchez Area Narrations**
2 **West Carroll Parish Narration**
3 **Monroe Area Narrations**
4 **Bienville Parish Narrations**
5 **Alexandria / Central Louisiana Narrations**

6 **Lafayette / Opelousas Area Narrations**
7 **Baton Rouge Area Narrations**

8 **New Orleans Area Narrations**

CONCORDIA PARISH

NATCHEZ AREA

Cotton pickers on Somerset Plantation
Courtesy of Historic Natchez Foundation

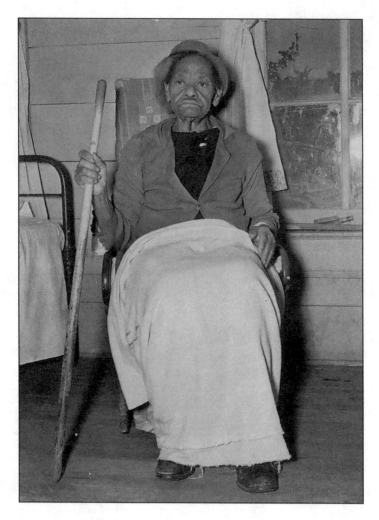

Mary Reynolds
Courtesy of Library of Congress, Manuscript Division, Image #mesnp 163236

MARY REYNOLDS

Age: unknown
Concordia Parish, Louisiana

"My paw's name was Tom Vaughn and he was from the north, born free man and lived and died free to the end of his days. He wasn't no eddicated man, but he was what he calls himself a piano man. He told me once he lived in New York and Chicago and he built the insides of pianos and knew how to make them play in tune. He said some white folks from the south told he if he'd come with them to the south he'd find a lot of work to do with pianos in them parts, and he come off with them.

"He saw my maw on the Kilpatrick place and her man was dead. He told Dr. Kilpatrick, my massa, he'd buy my maw and her three chillun with all the money he had, iffen he'd sell her. But Dr. Kilpatrick was never one to sell any but the old niggers who was past workin' in the fields and past their breedin' times. So my paw marries my maw and works the fields, same as any other nigger. They had six gals: Martha and Pamela and Josephine and Ellen and Katherine and me.

"I was born same time as Miss Sara Kilpatrick. Dr. Kilpatrick's first wife and my maw come to their time right together. Miss Sara's maw died and they brung Miss Sara to suck with me. It's a thing we ain't never forgot. My maw's name was Sallie and Miss Sara allus looked with kindness on my maw.

"We sucked till we was a fair size and played together, which wasn't no common thing. None the other li'l niggers played with the white chillun. But Miss Sara loved me so good.

"I was jus' bout big nough to start playin' with a broom to go bout sweepin' up and not even half doin' it when Dr. Kilpatrick sold me. They was a old white man in Trinity and his wife died and he didn't have chick or child or slave or nothin'. Massa sold me cheap, cause he didn't want Miss Sara to play with no nigger young'un. That old man bought me a big doll and went off and left me all day, with the door open. I jus' sot on the floor and played with that doll. I used to cry. He'd come home and give me somethin' to eat and then go to bed, and I slep' on the foot of the bed with him. I was scart all the time in the dark. He never did close the door.

"Miss Sara pined and sickened. Massa done what he could, but they wasn't no peartness in her. She got sicker and sicker, and massa brung nother doctor. He say, 'You li'l gal is grievin' the life out her body and she sho' gwine die iffen you don't do somethin' bout it.' Miss Sara says over and over, 'I wants Mary.' Massa say to the doctor, 'That a li'l nigger young'un I done sold.' The doctor tells him he better git me back iffen he wants to save the life of his child. Dr. Kilpatrick has to give a big plenty more to git me back than what he sold me for, but Miss Sara plumps up right off and grows into fine health.

"Then massa marries a rich lady from Mississippi and

they has chillun for company to Miss Sara and seem like for a time she forgits me.

"Massa Kilpatrick wasn't no piddlin' man. He was a man of plenty. He had a big house with no more style to it than a crib, but it could room plenty people. He was a medicine doctor and they was rooms in the second story for sick folks what come to lay in. It would take two days to go all over the land he owned. He had cattle and stock and sheep and more'n a hundred slaves and more besides. He bought the bes' of niggers near every time the spec'lators come that way. He'd make a swap of the old ones and give money for young ones what could work.

"He raised corn and cotton and cane and taters and goobers, sides the peas and other feedin' for the niggers. I member I helt a hoe handle mighty onsteady when they put a old woman to larn me and some other chillun to scrape the fields. That old woman would be in a frantic. She'd show me and then turn bout to show some other li'l nigger, and I'd have the young corn cut clean as the grass. She say, 'For the love of Gawd, you better larn it right, or Solomon will beat the breath out you body.' Old man Solomon was the nigger driver.

"Slavery was the worst days was ever seed in the world. They was things past tellin', but I got the scars on my old body to show to this day. I seed worse than what happened to me. I seed them put the men and women in the stock with they hands screwed down through holes in the board and they feets tied together and they naked behinds to the world. Solomon the . . . overseer beat them with a big whip and massa look on. The niggers better not stop in the fields when they hear them yellin'. They cut the flesh most to the bones and some they was when they taken them out of stock and put them on the beds, they never got up again.

"When a nigger died they let his folks come out the fields to see him afore he died. They buried him the same day, take a big plank and bust it with a ax in the middle nough to bend it back, and put the dead nigger in betwixt it. They'd cart them down to the graveyard on the place and not bury them deep nough that buzzards wouldn't come circlin' round. Niggers mourns now, but in them days they wasn't no time for mournin'.

"The conch shell blowed afore daylight and all hands better git out for roll call or Solomon bust the door down and get them out. It was work hard, git beatin's and half fed. They brung the victuals and water to the fields on a slide pulled by a old mule. Plenty times they was only a half barrel water and it stale and hot, for all us niggers on the hottes' days. Mostly we ate pickled pork and corn bread and peas and beans and taters. They never was as much as we needed.

"The times I hated most was pickin' cotton when the frost was on the bolls. My hands git sore and crack open and bleed. We'd have a li'l fire in the fields and iffen the ones with tender hands couldn't stand it no longer, we'd run and warm our hands a li'l bit. When I could steal a tater, I used to slip it in the ashes and when I'd run to the fire I'd take it out and eat it on the sly.

"In the cabins it was nice and warm. They was built of pine boardin' and they was one long row of them up the hill back of the big house. Near one side of the cabins was a fireplace. They'd bring in two, three big logs and put on the fire and they'd last near a week. The beds was made out of puncheons fitted on holes bored in the wall, and planks laid cross them poles. We had tickin' mattresses filled with corn shucks. Sometimes the men build chairs at night. We didn't know much bout havin' nothin', though.

"Sometimes massa let niggers have a li'l patch. They'd raise taters or goobers. They liked to have them to help fill out on the victuals. Taters roasted in the ashes was the best tastin' eatin' I ever had. I could die better satisfied to have jus' one more tater roasted in hot ashes. The niggers had to work the patches at night and dig the taters and goobers at night. Then if they wanted to sell any in town they'd have to git a pass to go. They had to go at night, cause they couldn't ever spare a hand from the fields.

"Once in a while they's give us a li'l piece of Sat'day evenin' to wash out clothes in the branch. We hanged them on the ground in the woods to dry. They was a place to wash clothes from the well, but they was so many niggers all couldn't get round to it on Sundays. When they'd git through with the clothes on Sat'day evenin's the niggers which sold they goobers and taters brung fiddles and guitars and come out and play. The others clap they hands and stomp they feet and we young'uns cut a step round. I was plenty biggity and like to cut a step.

"We was scart of Solomon and his whip, though, and he didn't like frolickin'. He didn't like for us niggers to pray, either. We never heared of no church, but us have prayin' in the cabins. We'd set on the floor and pray with our heads down low and sing low, but if Solomon heared he'd come and beat on the wall with the stock of his whip. He'd say, 'I'll come in there and tear the hide off you backs.' But some the old niggers tell us we got to pray to Gawd[,] that he don't think different of the blacks and the whites. I know that Solomon is burnin' in hell today, and it pleasures me to know it.

"Once my maw and paw taken me and Katherine after night to slip to nother place to a prayin' and singin'. A nigger man with white beard told us a day am comin' when niggers only be slaves of Gawd.

"We prays for the end of Trib'lation and the end of beatin's and for shoes that fit our feet. We prayed that us niggers could have all we wanted to eat and special for fresh meat. Some the old ones say we have to bear all, cause that all we can do. Some say they was glad to the time they's dead, cause they'd rather rot in the ground than have the beatin's. What I hated most was when they'd beat me and I didn't know what they beat me for, and I hated they strippin' me naked as the day I was born.

"When we's comin' back from that prayin', I thunk I heared the nigger dogs and somebody on horseback. I say, 'Maw, its them nigger hounds and they'll eat us up.' You could hear them old hounds ... abayin'. Maw listens and say, 'Sho nough, them dogs am runnin' and Gawd help us!' Then she and paw talk and they take us to a fence corner and stands us up gainst the rails and say don't move and if anyone comes near, don't breathe loud. They went to the woods, so the hounds chase them and not git us. Me and Katherine stand there, holdin' hands, shakin' so we can hardly stand. We hears the hounds come nearer, but we don't move. They goes after paw and maw, but they circles round to the cabins and gits in. Maw say its the power of Gawd.

"In them days I weared shirts, like all the young'uns. They had collars and come below the knees and was split up the sides. That's all we weared in hot weather. The men weared jeans and women gingham. Shoes was the worstes' trouble. We weared rough russets when it got cold, and it seem powerful strange they'd never git them to fit. Once when I was a young gal, they got me a new pair and all brass studs in the toes. They was too li'l for me, but I had to wear them. The trimmin's cut into my ankles and them places got mis'ble bad. I rubs tallow in them sore places and wrops rags around them and my sores got worser and worser. The scars are there to this day.

"I wasn't sick much, though. Some the niggers had chills and fever a lot, but they hadn't discovered so many diseases then as now. Dr. Kilpatrick give sick niggers ipecac and asafoetide [asafetida] and oil and turpentine and black fever pills.

"They was a cabin called the spinnin' house and two looms and two spinnin' wheels goin' all the time, and two nigger women sewing all the time. It took plenty sewin' to make all the things for a place so big. Once massa goes to Baton Rouge and brung back a yaller girl dressed in fine style. She was a seamster nigger. He builds her a house way from the quarters and she done fine sewin' for the whites. Us niggers knowed the doctor took a black woman quick as he did a white and took any on his place he wanted, and he took them often. But mostly the chillun born on the place looked like niggers. Aunt Cheyney allus say four of hers were massas, but he didn't give them no mind. But this yaller gal breeds so fast and gits a mess of white young'uns. She larnt them fine manners and combs out they hair.

"Onct two of them goes down the hill to the doll house where the Kilpatrick chillun am playin'. They wants to go in the dollhouse and one the Kilpatrick boys say, 'That's for white chillun.' They say, 'We ain't no niggers, cause we got the same daddy you has, and he comes to see us near every day and fotches us clothes and things from town.' They is fussin' and Missy Kilpatrick is listenin' out her chamber window. She heard them white niggers say, 'He is our daddy and we call him daddy when he comes to our house to see our mama.'

"When massa come home that evenin' his wife hardly say nothin' to him, and he ask her what the matter and she tells him, 'Since you asks me, I'm studyin' in my mind bout them white young'uns of that yaller nigger wench from Baton Rouge.' He say, 'Now, honey, I fotches that gal jus' for you, cause she a fine seamster.' She say, 'It look kind of funny they got the same kind of hair and eyes as my chillun and they got a nose looks like yours.' He say, 'Honey, you jus' payin' tention to talk of li'l chillun that ain't got no mind to what they say.' She say, 'Over in Mississippi I got a home and plenty with my daddy and I got that in my mind.'

"Well, she didn't never leave and massa bought her a fine new span of surrey hosses. But she don't never have no more chillun and she ain't so cordial with the massa. Margaret, that yellow gal, has more white young'uns, but they don't never go down the hill no more to the big house.

"Aunt Cheyney was jus' out of bed with a sucklin' baby one time, and she run away. Some say that was nother baby of massa's breedin'. She don't come to the house to nurse her baby, so they misses her and old Solomon gits the nigger hounds and takes her trail. They gits near her and she grabs a limb and tries to hist herself in a tree, but them dogs grab her and pull her down. The men hollers them onto her, and the dogs tore her naked and et the breasts plumb off her body. She got well and lived to be a old woman, but nother woman has to suck her baby and she ain't got no sign of breasts no more.

"They give all the niggers fresh meat on Christmas and a plug tobacco all round. The highes' cotton picker gits a suit of clothes and all the women what had twins that year gits a outfittin' of clothes for the twins and a double, warm blanket.

"Seems like after I got bigger, I member more'n more niggers run away. They's most allus cotched. Massa used to hire out his niggers for wage hands. One time he hired me and a nigger boy, Turner, to work for some ornery white trash name of Kidd. One day Turner goes off and don't come back. Old man Kidd say I knowed bout it, and he tied my wrists together and stripped me. He hanged me by the wrists from a limb on a tree and spraddled my legs around the trunk and tied my feet together. Then he beat me. He beat me worser than I ever been beat before and I faints dead away. When I come to I'm in bed. I didn't care so much iffen I died.

"I didn't know bout the passin' of time, but Miss Sara come to me. Some white folks done git word to her. Mr. Kidd tries to talk hisself out of it, but Miss Sara fotches me home when I'm well enough to move. She took me in a cart and my maw takes care of me. Massa looks me over good and says I'll git well, but I'm ruint for breedin' chillun.

"After while I taken a notion to marry and massa and missy marries us same as all the niggers. They stands inside the house with a broom held crosswise of the door and we stands outside. Missy puts a li'l wreath on my head they kept there and we steps over the broom into the house. Now, that's all they was to the marryin'. After freedom I gits married and has it put in the book by a preacher.

"One day we was workin' in the fields and hears the conch shell blow, so we all goes to the back gate of the big house. Massa am there. He say, 'Call the roll for every nigger big nough to walk, and I wants them to go to the river and wait there. They's gwine be a show and I wants you to see it.' They was a big boat down there, done built up on the sides with boards and holes in the boards and a bi[g] gun barrel stickin' through every hole. We ain't never seed nothin' like that. Massa goes up the plank onto the boat and comes out on the boat porch. He say, 'This am a Yankee boat.' He goes inside and the water wheels starts movin' and that boat goes movin' up the river and they says it goes to Natches [Natchez, Mississippi].

"The boat wasn't more'n out of sight when a big drove of sojers comes into town. They say they's Fed'rals. More'n half the niggers goes off with them sojers, but I goes on back home cause of my old mammy.

"Next day them Yankees is swarmin' the place. Some the niggers wants to show them somethin'. I follows to the woods. The niggers shows them sojers a big pit in the ground, bigger'n a big house. It is got wooden doors that lifts up, but the top am sodded and grass growin' on it, so you couldn't tell it. In that pit is stock, hosses and cows and mules and money and chinaware and silver and a mess of stuff them sojers takes.

"We jus' sot on the place doin' nothin' till the white folks comes home. Miss Sara come out to the cabin and say she wants to read a letter to my mammy. It come from Louis Carter, which is brother to my mammy, and he done follow the Fed'rals to Galveston [Texas]. A white man done write the letter for him. It am tored in half and massa done that. The letter say Louis am workin' in Galveston and wants mammy to come with us, and he'll pay our way. Miss Sara say massa swear, 'Damn Louis Carter. I ain't gwine tell Sallie nothin',' and he starts to tear the letter up. [B]ut she won't let him, and she reads it to mammy.

"After a time massa takes all his niggers what wants to Texas with him and mammy gits to Galveston and dies there. I goes with massa to the Tennessee Colony and then to Navasota [both in Texas]. Miss Sara marries Mr. T. Coleman and goes to El Paso. She wrote and told me to come to her and I allus meant to go.

"My husband and me farmed round for times, and then I done housework and cookin' for many years. I come to Dallas and cooked seven year for one white family. My husband died years ago. I guess Miss Sara been dead these long years. I allus kep' my years by Miss Sara's years, count we is born so close.

"I been blind and mos' helpless for five year. I'm gittin' might enfeeblin' and I ain't walked outside the door for a long time back. I sets and members the times in the world. I members now clear as yesterday things I forgot for a long time. I members bout the days of slavery and I don't [be]lieve they ever gwine have slaves no more on this earth. I think Gawd done took that burden offen his black chillun and I'm aimin' to praise him for it to his face in the days of Glory what ain't so far off."

SILAS SPOTFORE

Age: 85
1804 Franklin Street, McDonoghville, Louisiana
Interviewer: Flossie McElwee

[The nineteenth-century Irish, Italian, and German community of McDonoghville, where Silas Spotfore was interviewed, was on the west bank of the Mississippi across the river from New Orleans. It has since been absorbed by the cities of Algiers and Gretna. The historical cemetery still exists.]

"I wuz born in Mississippi, at Fort Adams, de yr. of 1855. I's been here 40 yrs. My master name wuz Johnson[,] de ole madam name Miss Betsy Johnson. He owned a big plantation—he had a heap of slaves. Us raised cotton, corn, 'taters—de most work I ever done wuz to tend the hogs, sheeps, shuck corn, and things around the yard. We never did have very much to eat. It wuz a big family of us. I think dare is 11 chillums. I don't know where none of them are at, if dey is living are [or] dead.

"Oh yes, we had a certain time to go to bed and to get up. Before I wuz big enough to do anything, dare wuz a old nigger 'oman who was not able to do anything else, and she minded all the chaps while the older folks worked.

"Dey ring the bell fo' [before] day dot meant for everybody to be up. We had 'lasses an hoe cake for breakfast, sometimes meat.

"We allus cooked on de fireplace in black pots and skilets [sic].

"The carpenter made de beds we slept on, de mattresses were made out of corn shucks—looked something like bunks.

"Never did know what it wuz to wear pants. I wore long shirts until I was all most grown. We only had two of them a year, and dey had to last.

"I know for Christmas de ole messus allus give us a biscuit and a apple. We tho't dat wuz something.

"De older people wore red russet shoes[. D]ey were made on de plantation. (For Sunday) I use to have mocassins [sic] to wear in winter time. I know I've been out minding the sheep and hogs, it would be so cold until the ice cycle [icicles] would be breaking the trees down, and I would have to be out in de weather.

"Oh! when dey went to get married, dey would not asks de pa and ma, dey would ask de Boss and de ole missus about it. If dey said it wuz all right, dey read some kind of writing on a paper and dey wuz married. Den, if one of de other wuz daid dey got another husband. I never member seeing any slaves sold.

"I saw de Yankee soldiers, dey come in to my misses' houses, sat de bed on fire. Gess de house would have fumed up if my missus had not come threw [*sic*] and put de fire out behind dem.

"I knows dey went to de dairy, drink all de milk dey could hold, den poured out what wuz left. I never will forget how skeared I felt. Dey took ull de mules dat could be any use to dem—that when de battle at Port Hudson wuz fought [May–July 1863].

"My missus and boss both were cruel for I know how dey had dem poor nigger beat. I seed my grandma whipped until she had scars on her dat wuz dare when I got grown. My other grandma got branded with hot irons.

"When dey would be in de fields, the driver wuz allus over dem with a bull whip and he sho' didn't mind using it.

"My ma allus got up, cooked breakfast, fixed de dinner, and carried it to de fields in tin buckets. One of de old driver name was Noel Cristin—he sho' was cruel. Dey didn't work on Sunday. If they went of[f] de plantation, they was checked out and on Sunday night, the overseer would come through the quarter and see if dey wuz all in. If dare was any missing, it was just too bad, dey was whipped with bull whips—from 150 to 250 licks at one time. Den had to go to work. I tells the young nigger now about, it, dey don't seem to believe me. Never knew what school was, no church or nothing like that. Once in awhile, dey would have a little singing in the quatus, but you musn't call on the Law'd too much. I sho' is glad all dem days are over! Some of the 'omens sewed, some worked around the field, some at the house. My pa was a bootblack, he made de mocassins [*sic*] out of cowhide. When they got wet, dey was so hard you could hardly get your foot in dum. Oh, about de day we got sat free, us did not know what to do. Our missus said we could stay but my pa didn't want to. We hung around for a few days, den pa went to work for something to eat. You see, we didn't have a thing[,] left empty handed with nothing and, besides people was ignorant. Dey didn't have no sense like dey do now, I know.

"I knows my ma worked plenty weeks just for a peck of meal, and four lbs. of meat. Peoples would not do that now. Dis younger generation better be thankful dey got good government now and a good President."

VICTORIA WILLIAMS

Age: unknown
1810 Lowerline, New Orleans, Louisiana
Interviewer: Posey
February 27, 1941

"I was born in slavery time but I was too little to remember much. We belonged to Marse Sam McGehee in Liberty, Miss.

"I heard my parents say he had a mean overseer who didn't like Pa and was brutal to him, when Marse heard it he turned him off.

"Once when he was whipping him I heard my Pa say 'Pray Marster oh oh oh!' and I was a-crying, everytime he said this, it looked like the licks came a-faster and like they would never stop. He had a trough made and had the victuals put in it, and all had to eat together down the line.

"But God was in the plan just as He said He would be and out of tribulations He brought us out of the dark valley and made us all free, and equal human beings. Now we have the chance and education is a grand thing, if the Negro can take it without its turning his head.

"You see even when slaves were tortured they never forgot to pray. You know He said: 'He that believeth in me, I shall in no wise cast out' and God never made a promise that He did not keep.

"I got converted when I was young and I've never backslided.

"We uster sing from our hearts and not from books like they do now. La! if they heard us sing like that now they'd think we were crazy.

"I remember when one got religion we'd clap our hands and sing: 'Shout sister Phreeny, shout, shout sister Phreeny, shout!' and then she sang:

> It'll take more'n two to hol' me!
> And even that can't hold me
> I'll shout and shout
> O! Sis' Phreeny'll shout!

"Then everybody took hands with her in the lead and shouted. O, them was the days!

"And it generally took more than one man to hold a sister when she got converted and maybe she didn't want a certain one to do it, so she would sing:

" 'I don't want Brer' Jim to hold me. I want Brer' Dick to hold me!'

"In old time women wore waterfalls [a hairstyle or wig resembling a waterfall]. They don't do it now and sometimes they'd sing:

> You may tetch my hat
> You may tetch my shawl
> But don't you tetch my waterfall.

"This is a great day and I'm glad I lived to be in it. From the darkness into the light I can see the wisdom of it all—we were prepared through trials and tribulations to stand alone, but we should never forget that fiery path our parents trod.

"Lord God of Hosts be with us yet. Lest we forget, lest we forget."

WEST CARROLL PARISH

During the antebellum period, it was determined that Native American mounds located on Poverty Point Plantation in West Carroll Parish dated back to 1600 B.C. It has also been documented that Native Americans were among the first slaves in Louisiana. Today, Poverty Point has been nominated for recognition as a UNESCO World Heritage Site.
Bird Mound. Courtesy of Louisiana Office of State Parks

EDWARD ASHLEY

Age: 83
Interviewer: Michinard
June 15, 1940

Edward Ashley, now about eighty-three years of age, related the following story. Robert Ashley, his wife, and son Edward, were slaves of Mr. Henry Goodrich.

Mr. Goodrich's plantation was at Lake Providence. He was a very wealthy man and a very kind one. It seems that Mr. Goodrich weighed eight hundred pounds. It required four men to raise him from a chair.

On Christmas day, Mr. Goodrich would give money, turkeys and chickens, to all the colored families on his place. Should the house girl fail to obey an order, the Master gave her two or three licks with a strap, that was the extent of her punishment.

Mr. Goodrich had a big orchard. Should a slave desire an apple or a pear, he would have to say, "Marse, may I have a pear?" He gave nothing if you failed to call him "Marse."

Edward's father was the keeper of the toll gate at

Goodrich landing. The gate was from the plantation to the levee. The fare was a dollar.

One night, when Robert and his family were assembled in his cabin, someone knocked at the door. On opening, they were confronted with two men, who asked to be sheltered for the night and to put their horses in the stable to be fed. Robert hesitated, then one of the men said, "I am Jesse James, you know what crimes I have committed. I need shelter for myself, brother and horses[. N]ow if you refuse me [I] will leave you here dead."

Jesse James claimed he had not slept in twenty nights, ducking here and there. He then asked, "How far are the woods from here?" Edward, the son, answered, "One mile," Jesse looked at his brother and said, "That's the place, Frank!" Hearing Robert tell his wife, "That ain't Jesse James," he spoke up and said, "Just look at my hand, my thumb has been shot off." The brothers went to bed and slept. You could hear them snore clear across the road.

Next morning, after breakfasting, and after looking the horses over, they took their leave, warning Edward and his parents that if any one inquired about two men passing there to deny it.

After they had left, about 1 o'clock that day, two men came. [The interviewer here switches briefly to Edward's first-person account.] "So I'se said: 'Pa two more men at gate, I'se going to hide me,' so I went and hide. The men said, 'Did you see two men pass here?' Pa answered 'Yes.' 'Were they riding fast?' 'Yes. Who are you after all?'

" 'We are detectives from New York.' 'Well if you catch up with them you will have to do some shooting.' " [The interviewer here returns to a third-person telling.] The detectives were told that the men had inquired the distance to the woods. Hearing this, the detectives said, "Do you know they are the worst desperadoes in the country?"

That wood was a hundred miles deep and full of wild animals. Robert heard two days after that the detectives had been killed in a cotton field on the other side of the wood.

About two weeks later, Jesse and his brother came back to get Edward the son. When they refused to give him up, James had the family lined up, and said, "All right, I am going, but when I come back you will have that boy here."

It seems that the boy had run away from home. It must have been the next day that Bob Ford, a friend of Jesse, had shot him for a ransom of $50,000. . . . Bob Ford put up [in] a hotel with the money and he was later killed by Frank James, Jesse's brother.

MONROE AREA

Ouachita steamer headed to New Orleans, pictured at four-rivers confluence near Jonesville
Courtesy of Oliver Poole

MARY ISLAND

Age: 80
626 Nelson Street, El Dorado, Arkansas
Interviewer: Pernella M. Anderson
1937

"I was born in Union Parish, Louisiana in the year of 1857, so the white folks told me, and I am eighty years old. My mama died when I was two years old and my aunty raised me. She started me out washing dishes when I was four years old and when I was six she was learning me how to cook. While the other hands was working in the field I carried water. We had to cook out in the yard on an old skillet and lid, so you see I had to tote brush and bark and roll up little logs such as I could to keep the fire from one time of cooking to the other. I was not but six years old either. When I got to be seven years old I was cutting sprouts almost like a man and when I was eight I could pick one hundred pounds of cotton. When it rained and we could not go to the field my aunty had me spinning thread to make socks and cloth, then I had to card the bats and make the rolls to spin.

"My auntie was a slave and she lived in the edge of the field. Of course I was born a slave but didn't know much about it because my aunty did the bossing of me but I had a pretty hard time. Our wash tubs, water buckets, bread trays and such were made out of tupelo gum logs dug out with some kind of axe and when aunty would wash I had to use the battling stick. I would carry the wet clothes to a stump and beat them with that battling stick and we hung the clothes out on bushes and on the fence. We used water from a spring.

"In my young days all we wore was homespun and lowel [cotton cloth made in Lowell, Massachusetts, and shipped to plantations for slaves]. We lived in a log house with a dirt floor and the cracks was chinked with mud and our bed was some poles nailed against the wall with two legs out on the dirt floor, and we pulled grass and put [it] in the lowel bed tick. My aunty would get old dresses, old coats, and old pants and make quilts.

"I never went to school a day in my life. No, the back of my head has never rubbed against the walls of a schoolhouse and I never did go to Sunday School and I never did like it. And I didn't go to church until I was grown and the church that I did attend was called the Iron Jacket Church. Now they call it the Hard Shell Church. I believe in foot washing. I don't go to church now because there is no Hard Shell church close around here."

MANDY JOHNSON

Age: 92
607 Cypress Street, Pine Bluff, Arkansas
Interviewer: Mrs. Bernice Bowden

"This is me. I'se old and ain't no 'count. I was done grown when the war started. You know I was grown when I was washin' and ironin'. I stood right there and watched the soldiers goin' to war. I heared the big bell go b-o-n-g, b-o-n-g and everybody sayin' 'There's goin' to be a war, there's goin' to be a war!' They was gettin' up the force to go[,] bless your heart! Said they'd be back by nine tomorrow and some said 'I'm goin' to bring you a Yankee scalp.' And then they come again and want so many. You could hear the old drums go boom-boom. They was drums on this side and drums on that side and them drums was a talkin'! Yes'm, I'se here when it started—milkin' cows, washin' and cookin'. Oh, that was a time. Oh my Lord—them Yankees come in just like blackbirds. They said the war was to free the folks. Lots of 'em got killed on the first battle.

"I was born in Bastrop, Louisiana in February—I was a February colt.

"My old master was John Lovett and he was good to me. If anybody put their hands on any of his folks they'd have him to whip tomorrow. They called us old John's free niggers. Yes ma'm I had a good master. I ain't got a scratch on me. I stayed right in the house and nussed til I'm grown. We had a good time but some of 'em seed sights. I stayed there a year after we was free.

"I married durin' the war and my husband went to war with my uncle. He didn't come back and I waited three years and then I married again.

"You know they used to give the soldiers furloughs. One time one young man come home and he wouldn't go back, just hid out in the cane brake. Then the men come that was lookin' for them that 'exerted' [deserted] durin' the war and they waited till he come out for somethin' to eat and they caught him and took him out in the bayou and shot him. That was the onliest dead man I ever seen. I seen a heap of live ones.

"The war was gettin' hot then and old master was in debt. Old mistress had a brother named Big Marse Lewis. He wanted to take all us folks and sell us in New Orleans and said he'd get 'em out of debt. But old master wouldn't do it. I know Marse Lewis got us in the jail house in Bastrop and Mars John come to get us out and Marse Lewis shot him down. I went to my master's burial—yes'm, I did! Old mistress didn't let us go to New Orleans either. Oh Lordy, I was young them days and I wasn't afraid of nothin'.

"Oh ho! What you talkin' 'bout? Ku Klux? They come out here just like blackbirds. They tried to scare the people and some of 'em they killed.

"Yes Lord, I seen a heap. I been through a lot and I seen a heap, but I'm here yet. But I hope I never live to see another war.

"When peace was declared, old mistress say 'You goin' to miss me' and I sho did. They's good to us. I ain't got nothin' to do now but sit here and praise the Lord cause I gwine to go home some day."

ANNIE PARKS

Age: about 80
720 Pulaski Street, Little Rock, Arkansas
Interviewer: Samuel S. Taylor

"I was born and raised in Mer Rouge, Louisiana. That is between here and Monroe. I have been in Little Rock more than twenty-five years.

"My mother's name was Sarah Mitchell. That was her married name. I don't know what her father's name was. My father's name was Willie Clapp. He was killed in the first war—the Civil War. My father went to the war from Mer Rouge, Louisiana. I don't remember him at all. But that is what my mother told me about him. My mother said he had very good people. After he married my mother, old man Offord bought him. Offord's name was Warren Offord. They buried him while I was still there in Mer Rouge. He was a old-time Mason. That was my mother's master—in olden days.

"His grandmother took my mother across the seas with her. She (his grandmother) died on shipboard, and they throwed her body into the water. There's people denies it, but my mother told me it was so. Young Davenport is still living. He is a relative of Offords. My mother never did get no pension for my father."

Slave House and Occupation

"I was born in a log house. There were two doors—a front and a back—and there were two windows. My mother had no furniture 'cept an old-time wooden bed—big bed. She was a nurse all the time in the house. I heard her say she milked and waited on them in the house. My father's occupation was farming during slavery times.

"My mother always said she didn't have no master to beat on her. I like to tell the truth. My mother's master never let no overseer beat his slaves around. She didn't say just what we had to eat. But they always give us plenty, and there wasn't none of us mistreated.

"My father could have an extra patch and make a bale of cotton or whatever he wanted to on it. That was so that he could make a little money to buy things for hisself and his family. And if he raised a bale of cotton on his patch and wanted to sell it to the agent, that was all right."

Family

"I have a brother named Manual Clayton. If he's living still, he is younger than I am. He is the baby boy. I doesn't remember his father at all. I had five sisters with myself and two brothers. All of them were older than me except Manual. My mother had one brother and two sisters. Her brother's name was Lin Urbin. We always called him Big Buddy. He hasn't been so long died. My older brother is named Willie Clayton—if he's still living. Willie has a half dozen sons. He is my oldest brother. He lives way out in the country 'round Mer Rouge."

Freedom

"My mother said they promised to them money when they were freed. Some of them gave them something, and some of them didn't. My mother's folks didn't give her nothin'. The Government didn't give her nothin' either. I don't know just who told her she was free nor how. I don't remember myself."

Pattyrollers and Ku Klux

"I never heard much about pateroles [*sic*]. My mother said they used to whip you if they would catch you without a pass. I heard her talk about the Ku Klux after freedom."

Slave Worship

"My mother could always go to church on Sunday. Her slave-time preacher was Tom Johnson. Henry Soates and Matt Taylor were slavery-time preachers too. Old man Jacob Anderson too was a great preacher in slave time. There was a big arbor where they held church. That was outdoors. There was just a wood frame and green leaves laid over it. Hundreds of people sat under there and heard the gospel preached. The Offords didn't care how much you worshipped. If I was with them, I wouldn't have no trouble.

"In the winter time they had a small place to meet in. They build a church after the war. When I went home, eight or nine years ago, I walked all 'round and looked at all the old places."

Health

"You know my remembrance comes and goes. I ain't had no good remembrance since I been sick. I been mighty sick with high blood pressure. I can't work and I can't even go out. I'm 'fraid I'll fall down and get myself hurt or run over."

Support

"I don't get no help 'cept what my daughter gives me. I can't get no Old Age Pension. I never did get nothin' for my father. My mother didn't either. He was killed in the war, but they didn't give nobody nothing for his death. They told me they'd give me something and then they told me they wouldn't. I'm dependent on what my daughter does for me.

If I was back in Mer Rouge, I wouldn't have no trouble gettin' a pension, nor nothin' else."

Slave Marriages on the Offord Plantation

"My mother said they just read 'em together during slavery times. I think she said that the preacher married them on the Offord plantation. They didn't get no licenses."

Amusements

"They had quiltings and corn shuckings. I don't know what other amusements they had, but I know everything was pleasant on the Offord plantation.

"If slaves went out without a pass, my mother said her master wouldn't allow them to beat on them when they came in. They had plenty to eat, and they had substantial clothes, and they had a good fire."

Age

"I don't know how old I am. I was born before the war. My father went to the war when it begun. I had another brother that was born before the war. He doesn't remember nothin' about my father. I don't neither. I was too young."

Interviewer's Comments

Allowing for a year's difference between the two youngest children, and allowing that the boy was born immediately before the war, the girl could not be younger than seventy-eight. She could be older. She states facts as through her mother, but she seems to have experienced some of the things she relates. Her memory is failing. Failure to get pension or old age assistance oppresses her mind. She comes back to it again and again. She carries her card and her commodity order with her in her pocketbook.

She had asked me to write some letters for her when her daughter interfered and said that she didn't want it done. She said that she had told the case worker that her husband worked at Missouri Pacific Shop and that the case worker had asked her if she wouldn't provide for her mother. They live in a neat rented house. The mother weighs about a hundred and ten pounds and is tall. The daughter is about the same height but weighs about two hundred fifty. Time and again, the old lady tried to convey to me a message that she didn't want her daughter to hear, but I could not make it out. The daughter was belligerent, as is sometimes the case, and it was only by walking in the very middle of the straight and narrow path that I managed to get my story.

CHARLEY WILLIAMS

Age: 94
Tulsa, Oklahoma

"Iffen I could see out'n my old eyes, and I had me something to work with and de feebleness in my back and head would let me 'lone, I would have me plenty to eat in de kitchen all de time, and plenty tobaccy in my pipe, too, bless God!

"And dey wouldn't be no rain trickling through de holes in de roof, and no planks all fell out'n de flo' on de gallery neither, 'cause dis one old nigger knows everything about making all he need to git along! Old Master done showed him how to git along in dis world, jest as long as he live on a plantation, but living in de town is a different way of living, and all you got to have is a silver dime to lay down for everything you want, and I don't git de dime very often.

"But I ain't give up! Nothing like dat! On de days when I don't feel so feeble and trembly, I just keep patching 'round de place. I got to keep patching so as to keep it whar it will hold de winter out, in case I git to see another winter.

"Iffen I don't, it don't grieve me none, cause I wants to see Old Master again anyways. I reckon maybe I'll jest go up and ask him what he want me to do, and he'll tell me, and iffen I don't know how he will show me how, and I will try to do it to please him. And when I get done, I wants to hear him grumble like he used to say, 'Charley, you ain't got no sense but you is a good boy. Dis here ain't very good, but it'll do, I reckon. Git yourself a little piece o' dat brown sugar. But don't let no niggers see you eating it—if you do I'll whup your black behind!'

"Dat ain't de way it going be in Heaven, I reckon, but I can't sit here on dis old rottendy gallery and think of no way I better like to have it!

"I was a great big hulking buck of boy when the War came along and bust up everything, and I can 'member back when everybody was living peaceful and happy, and nobody never had no notion about no war.

"I was borned on the 'leventh of January, in 1843, and was old enough to vote when I got my freedom, but I didn't take no stock in all of that politics and goings on at that time, and I didn't vote until a long time after old Master passed away, but I was big enough before the War to re-member everything pretty plain.

"Old Master name was John Williams, and old Mistress name was Miss Betty, and she was a Campbell before she married. Young Missy was named Betty after her Mommy, and Young Master was named Frank, but I don't know who after. Our overseer was Mr. Simmons, and he was mighty smart and had a lot of patience, but he wouldn't take no talk nor foolishness. He didn't whup nobody very often, but he only had to whup 'em jest one time! He never did whup a nigger at de time de nigger done something, but he would wait until evening and have old Master come and watch

Charley Williams
Courtesy of Library of Congress, Manuscript Division, Image #130330

him do it. He never whupped very hard 'cept when he had told a nigger about something and promised a whupping next time and the nigger done it again. Then that nigger got what he had been hearing 'bout!

"De plantation was about as big as any. I think it had about three hundred acres, and it was about two miles northwest of Monroe, Louisiana. Then he had another not so big, two-three miles south of the big one, kind of down in the woodsy part along the White River bottoms. He had another overseer on that place and a big passel of niggers, but I never did go down to that one. That was where he raised most of his corn and shoats, and lots of sorghum cane.

"Our plantation was up on higher ground, and it was more open country, but still they was lots of woods all around and lots of the plantation had been whacked right out of de new ground and was full of stumps. Master's place was more open, though, and all in the fields was good plowing.

"The big road runned right along past our plantation, and it come from Shreveport and run into Monroe. There wasn't any town at Monroe in them days, jest a little cross-roads place with a general store and a big hide house. I think there was about two big hide houses, and you could smell that place a mile before you got into it. Old master had a part in de store, I think.

"De hide houses was jest long sheds, all open along de sides and kivered over with cypress clapboards.

"Down below de hide houses and de store was jest a little settlement of one or two houses, but they was a school for white boys. Somebody said there was a place where they had been an old fort, but I never did see it.

"Everything boughten we got come from Shreveport, and was brung in by the stage and the freighters, and that was only a little coffee or gun powder, or some needles for the sewing, or some strap iron for the blacksmith, or something like dat. We made and raised everything else we needed right on the place.

"I never did see any quinine till after I was freed. My mammy knowed jest what root to go out and pull up to knock de chills right out'n me. And de bellyache and de running off de same way, too.

"Our plantation was a lot different than some I seen other places, like way east of there around Vicksburg. Some of them was fixed up fancier but dey didn't have no more comforts than we had.

"Old Master come out into that country when he was a young man, and they didn't have even so much then as they had when I was a boy. I think he come from Alabama or Tennessee, and way back his people had come from Virginia, or maybe North Carolina, 'cause he knowed all about tobacco on the place. Cotton and tobacco was the long crops on his big place, and of course lots of horses and cattle and mules.

"De big house was made out'n square hewed logs, and chinked wid little rocks and daubed wid white clay, and kivered wid cypress clapboards. I remember one time we put on a new roof, and the niggers hauled up the cypress logs and sawed dem and frowed out de clapboards by hand.

"De house had two setting rooms on one side and a big kitchen room on the other, wid a wide passage in between, and den about was de sleeping rooms. They wasn't no stairways 'cepting on de outside. Steps run up to de sleeping rooms on one side from the passage way and on de other side from clean outside de house. Jest one big chimbley was all he had, and it was on the kitchen end, and we done all of the cooking in a fireplace dat was purty nigh as wide as de whole room.

"In de sleeping rooms, dey wasn't no fires 'cepting in brazers [*sic*] made out of clay, and we toted up charcoal to burn in 'em when it was cold mornings in the winter. Dey kept warm wid de bed clothes and de knitten clothes dey had.

"Master never did make a big gallery on de house, but our white folks would set out in the yard under de big trees in de shade. They was long benches made out'n hewed logs and all padded with gray moss and corn shuck padding, and dey set pretty soft. All de furniture in de house was home-made too. De beds had square posts as big around as my shank and de frame was mortised into 'em, and holes bored in de frame and home-made rope laced into [*sic*] make it springy. Den a great big mattress full of goose feathers and two-three comforts [*sic*] as thick as my foot wid carded wool inside! Dey didn't need no fireplaces!

"De quarters was a little piece from the big house, and dey run along both sides of de road that go to de fields. All one-room log cabins, but dey was good and warm, and everyone had a little open shed at the side whar we sleep in de summer to keep cool.

"They was two or three wells at the quarters for water and some good springs at de branch at de back of de fields. You could ketch a fish now and den in dat branch, but Young Master used to do his fishing in White River, and take a nigger or two along to do de work at his camp.

"It wasn't very fancy at de Big House, but it was mighty

pretty just de same, wid de gray moss hanging from de big trees, and de cool green grass all over de yard, and I can shet my old eyes and see it jest like it was before de War come along and bust it up.

"I can see Old Master setting out under a big tree smoking one of his long cheroots his tobacco nigger made by hand, and fanning himself wid his big wide hat another nigger platted out'n young inside corn shucks for him, and I can hear him holler at a big bunch of white geeses what's getting in his flower beds and see 'em string off behind de old gander towards the big road.

"When de day begin to crack de whole plantation break out wid all kind of noises, and you could tell what going on by de kind of noise you hear.

"Come de daybreak you hear de guinea fowls start po-tracking down at de edge of the woods lot, and den de roosters all start up 'round de barn and de ducks finally wake up and jine in. You can smell de sow belly frying down at de cabins in de 'row' to go wid de hoe cake and de buttermilk.

"Den pretty soon de wind rise a little, and you can hear a old bell donging way on some plantation a mile or two off, and den more bells at other places and maybe a horn, and pretty soon younder [*sic*] go old Master's old ram horn wid a long toot and den some short toots, and hear [*sic*] come de overseer down de row of cabins, hollering right and left, and picking the ham out'n his teeth with a long shiny goose quill pick.

"Bells and horns! Bells for dis and horns for dat! All we knowed was go and come by the bells and horns!

"Old ram horn blow to send us all to de field. We all line up, about seventy-five field niggers, and go by de tool shed and git our hoes, and maybe go hitch up de mules to de plows and lay de plows out on de side so de overseer can see iffen the points is shart [*sic*]. Any plow gits broke or de point gits bungled up on de rocks it goes to de blacksmith nigger, den we all git on down in de field.

"Den de anvil start dangling in de blacksmith shop; 'Tank! Deling-ding! Tank! Deling-ding!' and dat old bull tongue gitting straightened out!

"Course you can't hear de shoemaker awling and pegging, and de card spinners, and de old mammy sewing by hand, but maybe you can hear de old loom going 'frump, frump', and you know it all right iffen your clothes do be wearing out, cause you gwine get new britches purty soon!

"We had about a hundred niggers on dat place young and old, and about twenty on de little place down below. We could make about every kind of thing but coffee and gun powder dat our white folks and us needed.

"When we needs a hat we gits inside corn shucks and weave one out, and makes horse collars de same way. Jest tie two little soft shucks together and begin plaiting.

"All de cloth 'cepting the mistresses Sunday dresses come from de sheep to de carders and de spinners and de weaver, den we die it wid 'butternut' and hickory bark and indigo and other things and set it wid copperas. Leather tanned on de place made de shoes, and I never see a store boughten wagon wheel 'cepting among de stages and de freighters along de big road.

"We made purty, long back-combs out'n cow horn, and knitting needles out'n second hickory. Split a young hickory and put in a big wedge to prize it open, then cut it down and let it season, and you got good bent grain for wagon hames and chair rockers and such.

"It was jest like dat until I was grown and den one day come a neighbor man and say we in de War.

"Little while young Master Frank ride over to Vicksburg and jine de Sesesh [Confederate] army, but old Master jest go on lak nothing happen, and we all don't hear nothing more until along comes Sesesh soldiers and take most old Master's hosses and all of his wagons.

"I bin working on de tobacco, and when I come back to de barns everything was gone. I would go into the woods and get good hickory and burn it till it was all coals and put it out wid water to make hickory charcoal for curing de tobacco. I had me some charcoal in de fire trenches under de curing houses, all full of new tobacco, and overseer come and say bundle all de tobacco up and he going to take it to Shreveport and sell it befo' the soldiers take it too.

"After de hosses all gone and most de cattle and de cotton and de tobacco gone too, here come de Yankees and spread out all over de whole country. Dey had a big camp down below our plantation.

"One evening a big bunch of Yankee officers come up to de Big House and old Master set out de brandy in de yard and dey act purty nice. Next day de whole bunch leave on out of dat part.

"When de hosses all go Old Master sold all de slaves but about four, but he kept my pappy and mammy and my brother Jimmy and my sister Betty. She was named after old Mistress. Pappy's name was Charley and mammy's name was Sally. De niggers he kept didn't have much work without any hosses and wagons, but de blacksmith started in fixing up more wagons and he kept them hid in de woods until they was all fixed.

"Den along come some more Yankees, and dey tore everything we had up, an old Master was afeared to shoot at them on account his women folks, so he tried to sneak the fambly out but they kotched him and brung him back to de plantation.

"We niggers didn't know dat he was gone until we seen de Yankees bringing dem back. De Yankees had done took charge of everything and was camping in the big yard, and us was all down at the quarters scared to death but dey was jest letting us alone.

"It was night when the white folks tried to go away, and still night when the Yankees brung them back, and a house nigger come down to the quarters wid three-four mens in blue clothes and told us to come up to de Big House.

"De Yankees didn't seem to be mad wid old Master, but jest laughed and talked wid him, but he didn't take de jokes any too good.

"Den dey ask him could he dance and he said no, and dey told him to dance or make us dance. Dar he stood inside a big ring of dem mens in blue clothes, wid dey brass buttons shining in de light from de fire dey had in front of de tents, and he jest stood and said nothing, and it looked lak he wasn't wanting to tell us to dance.

"So some of us young bucks jest step up and say we was good dancers, and we started shuffling while de rest of de niggers pat.

"Some nigger women go back to de quarters and get de gourd fiddles and de clapping bones made out'n beef ribs, and bring dem back so we could have some music. We get all warmed up and get dance lak we never did dance befo! I speck we invent some new steps that night.

"We act lak we dancing for the Yankees, but we trying to please Master and old Mistress more than anything, and purty soon he begin to smile a little and we all feel a lot better.

"Next day de Yankees move on away from our place, and old Master start gitting ready to move out. We git de wagons we hid and de whole passel of us leaves out for Shreveport. Jest left the old place standing like it was.

"In Shreveport old Master git his cotton and tobacco money what he been afraid to have sent back to de plantation when he sell his stuff, and we strike out north through Arkansas.

"Dat was the awfulest trip any man ever make! We had to hide from everybody until we find out if dey Yankees or Sesesh and we go along little old back roads and up one mountain and down another, through de woods all de way.

"After a long time we git to the Missouri line, and kind of cut off through de corner of dat state into Kansas. I don't know how we ever git across some of dem rivers, but we did. Dey nearly always would be some soldiers around the fords, and dey would help us find de best crossing. Sometimes we had to unload de wagons and dry out de stuff what all got wet, and camp a day or two to fix up again.

"Purty soon we git to Fort Scott, and that was whar de roads forked ever whichaways. One went on north and one east and one went down into de Indian country. It was full of soldiers coming and going back and forth to Arkansas and Fort Gibson.

"We took de road on west through Kansas, and made for Colorado Springs.

"Fort Scott was all run down, and de old places whar dey used to have the soldiers was all fell in in most places. Jest old rackety walls and leaky roofs, and a big pole fence made out'n poles sot in de ground all tied together, but it was falling down too.

"They was lots of wagons all around what belonged to de army, hauling stuff for de soldiers, and some folks toll [*sic*] old Master he couldn't make us niggers go wid him, but we said we wanted to anyways, so we jest went on west across Kansas.

"When we got away on west we come to a fork, and de best road went kinda south into Mexico, and we come to a little place called Clayton, Mexico whar we camped a while and then went north.

"Dat place is in New Mexico now, but old Master jest called it Mexico. Somebody showed me whar it is on de map, and it looked lak it was a long ways off'n our road to Colorado Springs, but I guess de road jest wind off down dat ways at de time we went over it. It was jest two or three houses made out'n mud at dat time, and a store whar de soldiers and de Indians come and done trading.

"About dat time old Master sell off some of de stuff he been taking along, 'cause de wagons loaded too heavy for de mountains and he figger he better have de money than some of de stuff, I reckon.

"On de way north it was a funny country. We jest climb

all day long gitting up one side of one bunch of mountains, and all de nigger men have to push on the wheels while the mules pull and den scotch de wheels while de mules rest. Everybody but de white folks has to walk most de time.

"Down in de valleys it was warm like in Louisiana, but it seemed lak de sun aint so hot on de head, but it looked lak every time night come it ketch us up on top of one of dem mountains, and it almost as cold as in de winter time!

"All de niggers had shoes and plenty warm clothes and we wrop up at night in everything we can git.

"We get to Fort Scott again, and den de Yankee officers come and ask all us niggers iffen we want to leave old Master and stay dar and work, 'cause we all free now. Old Master say we can do what we please about it.

"A few of de niggers stayed dar in Fort Scott, but most of us say we gwine stay wid old Master, and we don't care iffen we is free or not.

"When we git back to Monroe to de old place us niggers git a big surprise. We didn't hear about it, but some [of] old Master's kin folks back in Virginia done come out dar and fixed the place up and kept it for him while we in Colorado, and it look 'bout as good as when we left it.

"He cut it up in chunks and put us niggers out on it on de halves, but he had to sell part of it to git de money to git us mules and tools and found to run on. Den after while he had to sell some more, and he seem lak he get old mighty fast.

"Young Master been in de big battles in Virginia, and he get hit, and den he get sick, and when he come home he jest lak a old man he was so feeble.

"About dat time they was a lot of people coming into dat country from de North, and dey kept telling de niggers dat de thing for dem to do was to be free, and come and go whar dey please.

"Dey try to get de darkies to go and vote but none us folks took much stock by what dey say. Old Master tell us plenty time to mix in the politics when de younguns git educated and know what to do.

"Jest de same he never mind iffen we go to de dances and de singing and sech. He allus lent us a wagon iffen we want to borry one to go in, too.

"Some de niggers what work for de white folks from de north act purty uppity and big, and come pestering 'round de dance places and try to talk up ructions amongst us, but it don't last long.

"De Ku Kluckers start riding 'round at night, and dey pass de word dat de darkies got to have a pass to go and come and to stay at de dances. Dey have to get de pass from de white folks dey work for and passes writ from de northern people wouldn't do no good. Dat de way de Kluckers keep de darkies in line.

"De Kluckers jest ride up to de dance ground and look at everybody's passes, and iffen some darky dar widout a pass or got a pass from de wrong man dey run him home, and iffen he talk big and won't go home, dey whop him and make him go.

"Any nigger out on de road after dark liable to run across the Kluckers, and he better have a good pass! All de dances got to bust up at about 'leven o'clock, too.

"One time I seen three-four Kluckers on hosses, all

wrapped up in white, and dey was making a black boy git home. Dey was riding hosses and he was trotting down de road ahead of 'em. Ever time he stop and start talking dey pop de whip at his heels and he start trotting on. He was so made [*sic*] he was crying, but he was gitting on down de road jest de same.

"I seen 'em coming and I gits out my pass young Master writ so I could show it, but when dey ride by one in front jest turns in his saddle and look back at tother [*sic*] men and nod his head, and they jist ride on by without stopping to see my pass. Dat man knowed me, I reckon. I looks to see iffen I knowed the hoss, but de Kluckers sometime swap dey hosses around amongst 'em, so de hoss maybe wasn't hisn.

"Dey wasn't very bad 'cause de niggers 'round dar wasn't bad, but I hear plenty of darkies git whopped in other places 'cause dey act up and say dey don't have to take off dey hats in de white stores and such.

"Any nigger dat behave hisself and don't go runing [*sic*] 'round late at night and drinking never had no trouble with de Kluckers.

"Young Mistress go off and git married, but I don't remember de name, cause she live off somewhar else, and de next year, I think it was, my pappy and mammy go on a place about five miles away owned by a man named Mr. Bumpus, and I go 'long wid my sister Betty and brother Jimmy to help 'em.

"I live around dat place and never marry until old mammy and pappy both gone, and Jimmy and Betty both married and I was gitting about forty year old myself, and den I go up in Kansas and work around until I git married at last.

"I was in Fort Scott, and I married Mathilda Black in 1900, and she is 73 years old now and was born in Tennessee. We went to Pittsburgh, Kansas, and lived from 1907 to 1913 when we come to Tulsa.

"Young Master's children writ to me once in a while and tell me how dey gitting 'long up to about twenty year ago, and den I never heard no more about 'em. I never had no children, and it looked lak my wife going out live me, so my mainest hope when I goes on is seeing mammy and pappy and old Master. Old overseer, I speck, was too devilish mean to be thar!

" 'Course I loves my Lord Jesus same as anybody, but you see I never hear much about Him until I was grown, and it seemed lak you got to hear about religion when you are little to soak it up and put much by it. Nobody could read the Bible when I was a boy, and dey wasn't no white preachers talked to the niggers. We had meetings sometime, but the nigger preacher jest talk about being a good nigger and 'doing to please the master,' and I allus thought he meant to please old Master, and I allus wanted to do dat anyways.

"So dat de reason I allus remember de time old Master pass on.

"It was about two years after de War, and old Master been mighty porely all de time. One day we was working in de Bumpus field and a nigger come on a mule and say old Mistress like to have us go over to de old place 'cause old Master mighty low and calling mine and Pappy's and Mammy's name. Old man Bumpus say go right ahead.

"When we get to de Big House old Master setting

propped up in de bed and you can see he mighty low and out'n his head.

"He been talking about gitting de oats stacked, 'cause it seemed to him lak it gitting gloomy-dark, and it gwine to rain, and hail gwine to ketch de oats in de shocks. Some nigger come running up to de back door wid an old horn [that] old Mistress sent him out to hunt up, and he blowed it so old Master could hear it.

"Den purty soon de doctor come to de door and say old Master wants de bell rung 'cause de slaves ought to be in from de fields, 'cause it gitting too dark to work. Somebody git a wagon tire and beat on it like a bell ringing right outside old Master's window, and den we all go up on de porch and peep in. Every body was snuffling kind of quiet, 'cause we can't help it.

"We hear old Master say, 'Dat's all right, Simmons. I don't want my niggers working in de rain. Go down to de quartes [*sic*] and see dey all dried off. Dey ain't got good sense, but dey all good niggers.' Everybody around de bed was crying, and we all was crying too.

"Den old Mistress come to de door and say we can go in and look at him if we want to. He was still setting propped up, but he was gone.

"I stayed in Louisiana a long time after dat, but I didn't care nothing about it, and it looked lak I am staying a long time past my time in dis world, 'cause I don't care much about staying no longer only I hates to leave Mathilda.

"But any time de Lord want me I am ready, and I likes to think when He ready He going to tell old Master to ring de bell for me to come on in."

BIENVILLE PARISH

French governor Jean-Baptiste Le Moyne de Bienville, "the Father of Louisiana." The earliest recorded manumission in Louisiana occurred in 1733 when Bienville freed two slaves he had owned for twenty-six years.

ISAAC ADAMS

Age: 87
Tulsa, Oklahoma

"I was born in Louisiana, way before the War. I think it was ten years before, because I can remember everything so well about the start of the War, and I believe I was about ten years old.

"My Mammy belonged to Mr. Sack P. Gee. I don't know what his real given name was, but it maybe was Saxon. Anyways we called him Master Sack.

"He was a kind of youngish man, and was mighty rich. I think he was born in England. Anyway his pappy was from England, and I think he went back before I was born.

"Master Sack had a big plantation ten miles north of Arcadia, Louisiana and his land run ten miles along both sides. He would leave in a buggy and be gone all day and still not get all over it.

"There was all kinds of land on it, and he raised cane and oats and wheat and lots of corn and cotton. His cotton fields was the biggest anywhere in that part and when chopping and picking times come he would get negroes from other people to help out. I never was no good at picking, but I was a terror with a hoe!

"I was the only child my Mammy had. She was just a young girl, and my Master did not own her very long. He got her from Mr. Addison Hilliard, where my pappy belonged. I think she was going to have me when he got her; anyways I come along pretty soon, and my mammy never was very well afterwards. Maybe Master Sack sent her back over to my pappy. I don't know.

"Mammy was the house girl at Mr. Sack's because she wasn't very strong, and when I was four or five years old she died. I was big enough to do little things for Mr. Sack and his daughter, so they kept me at the mansion, and I helped the house boys. Time I was nine or ten Mr. Sack's daughter was getting to be a young woman—fifteen or sixteen years old—and that was old enough to get married off in them days. They had a lot of company just before the War, and they had a whole bunch of house negroes around all the time.

"Old Mistress died when I was a baby, so I don't remember anything about her, but Young Mistress was a winder! She would ride horseback nearly all the time, and I had to go along with her when I got big enough. She never did go around the quarters, so I don't know nothing much about the negroes Mr. Sack had for the fields. They all looked pretty clean and healthy, though, when they would come up to the Big House. He fed them all good and they all liked him.

"He had so much different kinds of land that they could raise anything they wanted, and he had more mules and horses and cattle than anybody around there. Some of the boys worked with his fillies all the time and he went off to New Orleans ever once in a while with his race horses. He took his daughter but they never took me.

"Some of his land was in pasture but most of it was all open fields, with just miles of cotton rows. There was a pretty good strip along one side he called the 'old' fields. That's what they called the land that was wore out and turned back. It was all growed up in young trees, and that's where he kept his horses most of the time.

"The first I knowed about the War coming was when Mr. Sack had a whole bunch of whitefolks [*sic*] at the Big House at a function. They didn't talk about anything else all evening and then the next time they come nearly all their menfolks wasn't there—just the womenfolks. It wasn't very long till Mr. Sack went off to Houma with some other men, and pretty soon we knew he was in the War. I don't remember ever seeing him come home. I don't think he did until it was nearly all over.

"Next thing we know they was Confederate soldiers riding by pretty nearly every day in big droves. Sometimes they would come and buy corn and wheat and hogs, but they never did take any anyhow, like the Yankees done later on. They would pay with billets, Young Missy called them, and she didn't send to git them cashed but saved them a long time, and then she got them cashed, but you couldn't buy anything with the money she got for them.

"That Confederate money she got wasn't no good. I was in Arcadia with her at a store, and she had to pay seventy-five cents for a can of sardines for me to eat with some bread I had, and before the War you could get a can like that for two cents. Things was even higher then than later on, but that's the only time I saw her buy anything.

"When the Yankees got down in that country the most of the big men paid for all the corn and meat and things they got, but some of the little bunches of them would ride up and take hogs and things like that and just ride off. They wasn't anybody at our place but the womenfolks and negroes. Some of Mr. Sack's women kinfolks stayed there with Young Mistress.

"Along at the last the negroes on our place didn't put in much stuff—jest what they would need, and could hide from the Yankees, because they would get it all took away from them if the Yankees found out they had plenty of corn and oats.

"The Yankees was mighty nice about their manners, though. They camped all around our place for a while. There was three camps of them close by at one time, but they never did come and use any of our houses or cabins. There was lots of poor whites and Cajuns that lived down below us, between us and the Gulf, and the Yankees just moved into their houses and cabins and used them to camp in.

"The negroes at our place and all of them around there didn't try to get away or leave when the Yankees come in. They wasn't no place to go, anyway, so they all stayed on. But they didn't do very much work. Just enough to take care of themselves and their whitefolks.

"Master Sack come home before the War was quite over. I think he had been sick, because he looked thin and old and worried. All the negroes picked up and worked mighty hard after he come home, too.

"One day he went into Arcadia and come home and told us the War was over and we was all free. The negroes didn't know what to make of it, and didn't know where to go, so he told all that wanted to stay on that they could just go on like they had been and pay him shares.

"About half of his negroes stayed on, and he marked off land for them to farm and made arrangements with them to let them use their cabins, and let them have mules and tools. They paid him out of their shares, and some of them finally bought the mules and some of the land. But about half went on off and tried to do better somewhere else.

"I didn't stay with him because I was just a boy and he didn't need me at the house anyway.

"Late in the War my Pappy belonged to a man named Sander or Zander. Might been Alexander, but the negroes called him Mr. Sander. When pappy got free he come and asked me to go with him, and I went along and lived with him. He had a share-cropper deal with Mr. Sander and I helped him work his patch. That place was just a little east of Houma [Homer], a few miles.

"When my Pappy was born his parents belongs to a Mr. Adams, so he took Adams for his last name, and I did too, because I was his son. I don't know where Mr. Adams lived, but I don't think my Pappy was born in Louisiana, Alabama, maybe. I think his parents come off his boat, because he was very black—even blacker than I am.

"I lived there with my Pappy until I was about eighteen and then I married and moved around all over Louisiana from time to time. My wife give me twelve boys and five girls, but all my children are dead now but five. My wife died in 1920 and I come up here to Tulsa to live. One of my daughters takes care and looks out for me now.

"I seen the old Sack P. Gee place about twenty years ago, and it was all cut up in little places [pieces] and all run down. Never would have known it was one time a big plantation ten miles long.

"I seen places going to rack and ruin around—all the places I lived at in Louisiana—but I'm glad I wasn't there to see Master Sack's place go down. He was a good man done right by all his negroes.

"Yes, Lord, my old feets have been in mighty nigh every parish in Louisiana, and I seen some mighty pretty places, but I'll never forget how that old Gee plantation looked when I was a boy."

MARION JOHNSON

Age: unknown
Born and reared in Louisiana, interviewed in El Dorado,
Arkansas
Interviewer: Carol Graham

"…[The interviewee sang as he worked.] Good mornin', Missie! Glad to see you again. I is workin' on chairs again. Got these five to bottom for Mr. Brown and I sho can talk while I does this work.

"Ain't the sunshine pretty this mornin'? I prayed last night that the Lord would let today be sunny. I 'clare, Missie, hits rained so much lately till I bout decided me and all my things was goin' mildew. Yes'm, me and all-l-l my things. And I done told you I likes to set on my gallery to work. I likes to watch the folks go by. It seems so natchel like to set here and howdy with em.

"I been in this old world a long time, but just can recollect bein' a slave. Since Christmas ain't long past it sets me to thinkin' bout the last time old Sandy Clause come to see us. He brought us each one a stick of candy, a apple and a orange and he never did come to see us no more after that time cause we peeped. That was the last time he ever filt our stockin'. But you knows how chaps is. We just had to peep.

"You knows I was born and raised in Louisiana. I done told you that many times and I just wish you could see the vituals [*sic*] on old marster's table at Christmas time. Lawdy, but his table jes groaned with good things. Old Mistress had the cook cookin' for weeks before time it seemed to me. There was hams and turkeys and chickens and cakes of all kinds. They sho was plenty to eat. And they was a present for all the niggers on the place besides the heaps of pretty things the Marster's family got off the tree in the parlor.

"When I first began to work on the farm old master put me to cuttin' sprouts, then when I got big enough to make a field hand, I went to the field then. I done lots of kinds of work—worked in the field, split rails, built fences, cleared new ground and just anything old marster wanted me to do. I members one time I got a long old splinter in my foot and couldn't get it out, so my mammy bound a piece of fat meat round my foot and let it stay bout a couple days, then the splinter come out real easy like. And I was always cutting myself too when I was a chap. You know how careless chaps is. An soot was our main standby for cuts. It would close the gash and heal it. And soot and sugar is extra good to stop bleeding. Sometime, if I would be in the field too far away from the house or anyplace where we could get soot, we would get cobwebbs [*sic*] from the cotton house and different places to stop the bleeding. One time we wasn't close to neither and one the men scraped some felt off from a old black hat and put it on to stop the bleedin'.

"My feets was tough. Didn't wear shoes much till I was

grown. Went barefooted. My feet was so tough I could step on stickers and not feel em. Just to show how tough I was I used to take a blackberry limb and take my toes and skin the briars off and it wouldn't hurt my feets.

"Did I ever tell you about my first pair of breeches? I was about twelve then and before that I went in my shirt tail. I thought I was goin' to be so proud of my first breeches but I didn't like them. They was too tight and didn't have no pockets. They come just below my knees and I felt so uncomfortable like that I tore em off me. And did I get a lickin'? I got such a lickin' that when my next ones was made I was glad to put em on and wear em.

"I stayed round with marster's boys a lot, and them white boys was as good to me as if I had been their brother. And I stayed up to the Big House lots of nights so as to be handy for runnin' for old master or mistress. The big house was fine but the log cabin where my mammy lived had so many cracks in it that when I would sleep down there I could lie in bed and count the stars through the cracks. Mammy's beds was ticks stuffed with dried grass and put on bunks built on the wall, but they did sleep so good. I can most smell that clean dry grass now. Mammy made her brooms from broom sage, and she cooked on a fireplace. They used a oven and a fireplace up at the big house too. I never saw no cookstove till I was grown.

"I members one time when I was a little shaver I et too many green apples. And did I have the bellie ache, whoo-ee! And mammy poured cold water over hot ashes and let it cool and made me drink it and it sure cured me too. I members seein' her make holly bush tea, and parched corn tea too for sickness. Nother time I had the toothache and mammy put some axel [*sic*] grease in the hollow of the tooth and let it stay there. The pain stopped and the tooth rotted out and we didn't have to pull it.

"Whee! Did you see how that car whizzed round the corner? There warn't no cars in my young days. They had mostly two wheeled carts with shafts for the horse to be hitched in, and lots of us [hitched] oxen to them carts. I plowed oxen many-a-day and rode em to and from the field. Let me tell you, Missy, if you don't know nothin' bout oxen—they surely does sull on you—you beat em and the more you beat the more they sulls. Yes'm they sure sulls in hot weather, but it never gets too cold for em.

"Howdy, Parson. That sho was good preachin' Sunday. Yes suh, it was fine.

"That's the pastor of our church, an he sho preached two good sermons last Sunday. Sunday mornin' he preached 'Every kind of fish is caught in a net' and that night he preached 'Marvel not[,] you must be born again.' But that mornin' sermon, it capped the climax. Parson sho told em bout it. He say 'First they catch the crawfish, and that fish ain't worth much; anybody that gets back from duty or one which says I will and then won't is a crawfish Christian.' Then he say, 'The next is a mudcat; this kind of fish likes dark trashy places. When you catch em you won't do it in front water; it likes back water and wants to stay in mud. That's the way with some people in church. You can't never get them to the front for nothin'. You has to fish deep for them. The next one is the jellyfish. It ain't got no backbone to face the right thing. That the trouble with our churches today. Too many jellyfishes in em.' Next, he say is the goldfish—good for nothin' but to look at. They is pretty. That the way folks is. Some of them go to church just to sit up and look pretty to everybody. Too pretty to sing; too pretty to say amen! That what the parson preached Sunday. Well, I'm a full grown man and a full grown Christian, praise the Lord. Yes'm, parson is a real preacher. . . ."

ALEXANDRIA/
CENTRAL LOUISIANA

Alexandria on the Red River, pre–Civil War
Courtesy of the State Library of Louisiana

ADAM HALL

Age: 104
Maple Street, Alexandria, Louisiana

This negro, living on Maple Street, is one of the oldest negroes in this section of the state. According to his own statement and all records, Adam Hall was born on Flowerton Plantation on the Bayou Boeuf in 1833. The old negro is what may be called an aristocrat of his race due to his early life among the whites and the fact that he recalls the old South. He holds the white man in great respect. Physically, Adam is emaciated in form but has a mind that seems to be especially keen for one of his age. He has a face of a man of seventy and a countenance that invites confidence. He can no longer see and hear well, a fact which seems to worry him a great deal. Of open countenance and fearless eyes, he still sees humor in life and to hear him laugh as he holds his hands to his face makes one wonder at the qualities that he must have possessed when in the prime of life.

Adam remembers several incidents of his boyhood that he takes great pleasure in relating. One of the things of great importance to him in the old rule of his master, Charlie

Flowers: "Never get in too great a hurry, Adam, and you will live many years longer." The old negro to this day gives that rule as the reason for his long life and ability to continue actively until only a few years ago.

Uncle Adam states that his masters were all the finest men in the South, treating him so well that he had no desire for any change in life as most negroes have. In relating the experiences of his boyhood, he smiles as he says, "There was four of us, brothers in the Flowers' Home. The others hurried on in life and I am the only one left."

One of the experiences of [the] early life of Adam happened because of his disobedience to his mistress who warned him to keep away from the wild boys of his race. "I disobeyed her once and that like to have killed old Adam. I runned off with some bad boys living on the plantation near Lecompte and you know the first thing I knowed I was almost dead. I had my hip broke, my ankle broke, and my wrist broke. I couldn't move, couldn't get up and them boys runned off an' lef me, yes suh. One girl wouldn't leave me and got an ole feller from over de bayou to come to me. He come an' befo' he got dere started calling me.

" 'Adam,' he says, 'what's de matter with you?'

" 'Mah leg's broke. I can't get up.'

" 'No it ain't, Adam.'

"When he got dere he saw hit wuz. I wuz all crumpled up an' couldn't noways move. Well, suh, you talkin' about good kere. I got hit. Four doctors come to save Adam dat time. Dr. Compton, Dr. Cornal, Dr. Hardy, an' annuder one.

"Den de war come (Civil War) an wuz we scattered? Dere wuz eighteen of us in mah family an' only eight left.

I went to New Orleans wid mah marster and Mistus. We lived on the biggest street in New Orleans. Didn't I tell you I wuz de messenger boy on de plantation? Well, Suh, when de war come dey tuck [took] me to carry messages in de army. Hit wuz dangerous dem times. I seen 'em fall all 'round an' I kept traveling. Neber got hit in a place in de whole time I wuz in de fracus [sic].

"We wuz right dere in New Orleans when [Union] Gen'al [Nathaniel P.] Banks stormed de city. Such times I neber seed in all mah life. Den we come back here to farm some mo'. Fust thing we knowed de overseer had us move de rail fence fer dat new wire fence. Dr. Compton tole us what it wuz goin to be like, but de overseer wuz a persuadin' feller an' we put up de new fence an you see whut come of it.

"I 'member de steam boats on de Red River jist like yistiddy. Dere wuz de *John T. Moore*, de *Grand Duke* which wuz Cap'n Doty's boat. Den dere wuz de *Big Horn* and de Red River Mail Boat. De big ones couldn't come up de river, but we had some boats in dem days.

"Does I 'member Gen'al [Ulysses S.] Grant? Sho I members him. He had side-burns come way down de side of his face. I saw Gen'al Robert Lee. Dem wuz times in dis section I tell you. Frances Castle wuz de fust surveyor in dese parts long befo' Mr. Sylvester an' Mr. Bringhurst. Many a day I went wid dem in de swamps claring [sic] ways and runnin' lines. Why a man could live in dem days.

"I 'members de first bishop in de Catholic Church here. Old Father Bellier started de church in dis section. My little girl had a boil on her face. Hit wuz a terrible place an' de doctors wanted twenty-five dollars to cure it. One day I tuck her to the Catholic Church an' Father Bellier come out and looked at it. Den de Nurse come out and looked at it. She rubbed her hands ober de place an' when she finished, she said, 'Adam I am not charging you for this, but if you want to give a dollar for to help some other little girl, it will be fine.' Dat place got all right an' dem doctors didn't get no twenty-five dollars fer it nuther.

"De head an' de eye is de cornerstone of a man's life. If you jest trusts in God and believes in him in de right way you ain't goin' to fail in dis here life. Once a feller come down frum de North an' he was as crooked as a rams horn. Dats de way dey are. Don't eber deal wid crooked people, 'cause dey are as crooked as a rams horn an' putty soon you git dey way too. Don't eber deal wid fools, cause putty soon you be a fool too. It's jist lak I say. De Lord is the cause of all de good things a man gits in life. It ain't nothin' in ole Adam keepin' him here. Hit's de Lord's work dat I been here all dese years. You got to trus' him all de way tho' an' not jist half-way."

Uncle Adam is living with his son now and has been for the past several years. The wife of the son states that until about eight years ago Uncle Adam would get up long before them in the morning and not be back until late at night. His last work was trimming hedges and working yards for the residents of Alexandria. Some of his quiet spirit seems to have been imbued by those about him, giving sensitiveness of manner that is rarely found in negroes.

ISABELLA JACKSON

Age: 79
Born and reared near Bunkie, Louisiana, interviewed in
Tulsa, Oklahoma

"Boom . . . Boom! Boom . . . Boom! That's the way the old weaver go all day long when sister, Margaret, is making cloth for the slaves down on old Doc Joe Jackson's plantation in Louisiana.

"That was near the little place of Bunker [Bunkie], and it's my birthplace, and I guess where all Mammy's children were born because she was never sold but once and nobody but the old Doc ever did own her after she come to his place.

"He always say couldn't nobody get work out of Mammy but him, I guess that's just his foolery 'cause if she ain't no good the Old Doc most likely sell her to some of them white folks in Texas.

"That's what they done to them mean, no account slaves—just send them to Texas. Them folks sure knew how for to handle 'em!

"But I was talking about my sister, Margaret. I can still see her weaving the cloth—Boom . . . Boom!—and she hear that all day and get mighty tired. Sometimes she drop her head and go to sleep. The Mistress get her then sure. Rap her on the head with almost anything handy, but she hit pretty easy, just trying to scare her that's all.

"The old Master though, he ain't so easy as that. The whippings was done by the master[,] and the overseer just tell the old Doc about the troubles, like the old Doc say:

" 'You just watch the slaves and see they works and works hard, but don't lay on with the whip, because I is the only one who knows how to do it right!'

"Maybe the old Master was sickened of whippings from the stories the slaves told about the plantation that joined ours on the north.

"If they ever was a living Devil that plantation was his and the owner was It [*sic*]! That's what the old slaves say, and when I tell you about it see if I is right.

"That man got so mean even the white folks was scared of him, 'specially if he was filled with drink. That's the way he was most of the time, just before the slaves was freed.

"All the time we hear about slaves on that place getting whipped or being locked in the stock—that one of them things where your head and hands is fastened through holes in a wide board, and you stands there all the day and all the night—and sometimes we hears of them staying in the stock for three-four weeks if they trys to run away to the north.

"Sometimes we hears about some slave who is shot by that man while he is wild with the drink. That's what I'm telling about now.

"Don't nobody know what made the master mad at the

old slave—one of the oldest on the place. Anyway, the master didn't whip him; instead of that he kills him with the gun and scares the others so bad most of 'em runs off and hides in the woods.

"The drunk master just drags the old dead slave to the graveyard which is down in the corner away from the growing crops, and hunts up two of the young boys who was hiding in the barn. He takes them to dig the grave.

"The master stands watching every move they make, the dead man lays there with his face to the sky, and the boys is so scared they could hardly dig. The master keeps telling them to hurry with the digging.

"After while he tells them to stop and put the body in the grave. They wasn't no coffin, no box, for him. Just the old clothes that he wears in the fields.

"But the grave was too short and they start to digging some more, but the master stop them. He says to put back the body in the grave, and then he jumps into the grave hisself. Right on the dead he jumps and stomps 'til the body is mashed and twisted to fit the hole. Then the old nigger is buried.

"That's the way my Mammy hears it and told it to us children. She was a Christian and I know she told the truth.

"Like I said, Mammy was never sold only to Master Jackson. But she's seen them . . . slave auctions where the man, women and children was stripped naked and lines [*sic*] up so's the buyers could see what kind of animals they was getting for their money.

"My pappy' name was Jacob Keller and my mother was Maria. They's both dead long ago, and I'm waiting for the old ship Zion that took my Mammy away, like we use to sing of in the woods:

> It has landed my old Mammy,
> It has landed my old Mammy,
> Get on board, Get on board,
> 'Tis the Old Ship of Zion—
> Get on board!"

MANDY ROLLINS

Age: 110
Sonia Quarters, Alexandria, Louisiana
Interviewer: Rouceive Baham, Louisiana College student
1937

"My missus wuz Miss Delia Casson, whut wuz de dauter uv Marse Gen'al Thomas. Lawdy, all dese houses stands now on de land whar I usta wuk like a mule. Ise plowed, hoed, stripped cane, pulled con [corn], an mos' erething dat a man eber did. An' 'fo we wurked dis lan', I hepped annuder 'oman cut down de trees right whar dese cabins is now. My man uster go to de sugar mill ever Sunday and sell sirup [syrup] on Gen'al Thomas place. At night time he carried a water-bucket [*sic*] ub money to de house to Miss Delia. 'Lawdy,' she'd say, 'Its jes' a drap in de bucket along wid what you done brought.'

"Usses wore ole couse [coarse] lowell dresses and raw-hide shoes. Usses had plenty to eat like conbread, meat, 'lasses, etc. Arter I wuz freed I moved off and wurked by de day and Lawdy, I got as much as five dollars a day sometimes.

"Sho, usses had a church on de plan'ation! Usses couldn't

Caption: Mandy Rollins
Credit: Courtesy of State Library of Louisiana; Image #hp005953

do lak us wanted to whilst us wuz dar. Us allus had to hab a pass wh[e]n us wanted to visit usses frens on annuder place. An' when us wrot [*sic*] or had a letter wrot hit had to be sant [*sic*] by de fust passin' pusson [person] dat come by. Fudermore dar wuz tree [three] plan'ations, de 'Big', de 'Little', and de 'Scott Bottom'. Dar wuz a sick-house on de place and us had a cullud doctor. Dar wuz annuder oberseer named, 'Crookshank'. One wuz named 'Waters' and dey killed him. Mist Huff had six mens hanged fur hit 'fo Gen'al Thomas foun hit out. He claimed he could've sabed [saved] de mens ef he had knowed hit. I sho' wuz glad when de day come dat I wuz free!"

According to family records, the family sought Presidential assistance to stay the execution of these slaves.

LAFAYETTE/OPELOUSAS AREA

Cutting cane on Jefferson Island
Courtesy of the State Library of Louisiana

OCTAVIA FONTENETTE

Age: 86
4615 Camp Street, City [New Orleans]
Interviewer: Burke
March 11, 1940

Memory—that elusive thing which sometimes we have and sometime we have not—seems to be vividly alive and fresh in the mind of Octavia Fontenette, who lives to talk of the days through which she had watched six generations of her family pass. She is proud of her age and the heritage which seems to have been handed down from her mother's mother.

"I am the youngest one living of thirty-three children. Yes[,] suh, thirty-three children my mother had by three different husbands—eleven for each one. We were all born in New Iberia Parish and today I'm the youngest one living. I be eighty-seven years come next birthday. I got a sister living in New Iberia who's one hundred and eleven years old. My mother herself died when she was one hundred and eighteen. My husband died when he was seventy-seven. But, he didn't die a natural death. He was poisoned.

"I've got one sone [*sic*] living here in the City. His name is Walter Fontenette. He's working at the mattress factory. Walter is fifty-seven years old.

"Why I remember when I was a little girl back in New Iberia Parish. I was born right in the middle of slavery. But it was a funny thing. Our master was named Dr. Hatcher and he was one of the kindest men I know. He bought my mother and I was born on his plantation. Then five years before the war he set us free—signed papers and everything. But my mother and my father stayed on the next year to help with the crop. Then they stayed on the next year and the next until after the war. But they didn't want me to stay out there so they sent me to New Orleans. As a girl we used to have some good times because we were free and could do almost anything we wanted to. But the slaves on the other plantations didn't have it so easy. I know 'cause I used to sneak off and play in the fields. They didn't make us children work and we used to see the white master on the other farms beatin' their poor slaves. One day we saw them dig a big hole and make a poor woman get in it face down with her clo'es off and they beat her 'til she bled. We snuk [*sic*] off home and told the others about what we had seen. But they fussed at us and told us we better not never go over there again. And you know it was years after I found out why they made those women do that. They was pregnant.

"My folks didn't want me to be brought up out there so they sent me here when I was eighteen years old. Did I tell you ten or eighteen years before? Well, I remembers clearly—I kin remember too when the Yankees was here. All the gunboats was on the river and the soldiers was marching in and out but nobody was harmed, not that I know of.

"We moved down on St. Ann Street—Where? Between Rampart and Burgundy. That was when I was a big girl. Did I remember the Voodoo Queen? You's talkin' about that woman Marie Laveau ain't you? Why sure. We lived right across the street from her. Here's her house and here's our house. She was a fine Indian-looking woman and she would go about with her head up not meddling in anybody's business. Everybody used to talk and say things about her but we never used to pay any attention to see if it was true or not. We used to play with her children—Meme, Fidelia and Joe.

"We was all about the same ages. Maybe they was a little younger, but not much. We was big children but we didn't have anything else to do but play. But, I remember when Marie Laveau died. It musta been four years after we moved on St. Ann Street. I was about twenty-two years old. But I don't know nothing about how she died because we didn't have sense enough to notice nothing.

"But we lived downtown for thirty-three years and then moved uptown where I been livin' for forty-five years."

MARY ANN JOHN

Age: 85
Back highway [?], McDonoghville, Louisiana
Interviewer: McElwee
June 6, 1940

"I was ten years old when peace declared—on the 14th of February, I was eighty-five years old. I still get around good, though—lives right here by myself.

"Yaas mam I 'member a few things about slave times—

"Mr. Lizi, he was a Creole, dats who us belonged to. He stayed in Opelousas durin' slavery. Dis man sho did have some slaves! He raised cotton, corn, tatus. My ma use to work in de fields: she got, kind of sickly, so dey took her out and made a house servant of her.

"We eats on de house with our Boss—We allus had good grub. I had two sisters an' one brother—don't know if dey is still livin' or not.

"Ise been here in McDonoghville for fifty years.

"O yaas! I owns mah little place here.

"My pa's name was Alfred, Ma's name was Maria.

"What I knows, I was borned with, for I never went

to school a day in my whole life, I don't know 'A,' from 'B.' No, we never knowed whut church was until I was almos' growed.

"You see whut caused my ma to be sickly, I was de oldes' chile an' dey made her work too hard with de other children. One of my sisters was born right in de fields, dey jost dug two holes, one in de front and one in the back, she gets down in dat hole and gives birth to de baby, de baby jest rolls out in de hole. Den de boss has some one to take de baby to de house, an' makes my ma get up and keep right on hoeing—

"I never will forgit.

"I felt so sorry for dem poor people. I was not big enough to do much; you see I never was 'llowed in de fields. After that, they taken my ma out an' put her sewin' and doin' house work. You know my ma allus told me if we had not of been set free when us was, in about two years, they would of made me have a baby. They had a big ole husky man on de place dey waiold [*sic*] send all de gals to. If dey didn' want to go, dey give dem a lashin' an' made dem go; if dey did not git pregnant de first time dey was forced to go back. You see dat nigger didn' do a thing but got babies—you see dey allus sold dem. I was glad I was never forced to do any thing like that.

"I seed de Yankee sojers comin' down de road with dem swords a flashin', and de folks would run and cry. It sho was tryin' days den. Dat's about all I 'member.

"I peddles vegetables on de street here for forty years. My husband was a moss picker; never did have no trouble with no one but him, he was allus jealous of me, and dat is all de trouble I ever had.

"I never is been sick in my life; don' drink, smoke or use glasses.

"I can eat anything [I] want, I got 'ligion [religion] too—Baptist.

"I do 'member about pickin' fruit in dem days; it sho was plentiful.

"I can't 'member nothin' 'bout de clothes we wore, or nothin' dat been so long until its all done lef' me.

"I don' know nothin' about ghosts, witches or nothin' and no kinds of medicine.

"I quit singin' when I got 'ligion, all I ever sing is our church songs."

HENRY REED

Age: 86
304 Monroe Street, McDonoghville, Louisiana
Interviewer: Flossie McElwee

"I was borned in 1853, Saint Landry Parish, Opelousas. My maw's name was Margaret, Paw's name Lewis Rud [*sic*]. He got kilt during the war. We belonged to Governor Mouton [Alexandre Mouton was a United States senator and later governor of Louisiana from 1843 to 1846].

"I had two brothers. Nat was the oldest, I wuz the second child. My third brother had my father's name Lewis.

"After the sojers taken my pa to war, and we wuz sat [*sic*] free, my maw brung us to Morgan City. I never is seen my father any more. He died while in the service.

"I was a house servant and yard boy. Waited on the Marse and Missus. My Missus christen me in Saint Landry parish[.] Yes Mam, she allus fed me when I was hungry, we had milk, 'taters, possums. Wild duck and all kinds of good grub. In dem days you did not have to pay to hunt them.

"Us got our vegetables out of the Marse's garden, you see, us had worked and made dem.

"Dey give the older people shoes, us yonger [*sic*] folks

went bare feeted. Dey use to make uses [us] clothes, we allus had good clothes 'cause our Marse was the Governor.

"He had a big fine house. I think there was five in the family as well as I 'member. Oh Yes! [I]t was a large cotton plantation! They never did learn me to read and write.

"The white folks and Negro all went to the same church, we allus had holidays off.

"I was the yard boy and they did not allow me to go out. I never did 'member playing anything but marble[s]. When we got sick, dey allus had the family doctor with us.

"When the niggers wanted to have a little fun, dey would go to the back of the field and shoot craps. No indeed, dey did not have any money! They allus got under a big magnolia tree, but the old marse catched up with 'em—he had a spy glass. My maw saw it one day while she was making the beds. You see he would go up stairs and look out de window, and when dem niggers comes in, he would give them all a good lashing. So my maw posted them and dey soon stopped all that foolishness.

"[I w]as raised up with Creoles until 1865. When I got with the real American[s], I learned how to talk. You see, I was a Catholic then, but am a converted man now. I belong to the Baptist church. I had a good maw, she was the cause of me being converted. It is the faith you has got in the Lord dat gets you through this world.

"After being reborned again I believed in the Heavenly Father. What makes it bad today, people don't believe in the hereafter, you see God completed the world before he stopped.

"You know we got some where to spend eternity, it is a Heaven and Hell.

"I don't believe in lying, stealing—God ain't got no room for them.

"Oh yes, I'se a preacher, talk about when I was converted, De Lawd called me. There was no bigger sinner no where than me. I went around cussing all time. So the people got to telling me what a good Lawd we had, how good you felt, when you got 'legion [religion], so I said I wanted some of it too. So I found out you had to seek for life and salvation. De preacher axed me if I wanted 'legion. I told him 'Yes'. So I went down in the woods and got down on my knees. I axed the Lawd of [*sic*] there was such a thing as a God, but He did not seem to hear me, so I just kept on praying, got to where I could not eat or sleep, finally I see'd the sp'rit, and I'se had 'legion every since. Oh Yes! I preached to thousand of people at the Industrial Canal during the World War, stood in mud knee deep. All I know comes from God, for I can't read nor write, when I was converted people were scared of me. You know there was lots of 'omens left their chellums [children]. [W]hen the sojers come, I remember when some was throwed in the canal. I thank God my maw never left me. I was 40 yrs. old, when I married. The Welfare is helping us now. We should thank God for that!

"Well dis is my favorite song:

> Glory, Glory Hallelujah
> When I lay my burdens down
> When I lay my burdens down
> No more Monday, No more Tuesday
> Glory Glory Hallelujah, Howdy Jesus Howdy
> No more sorrows, No more weeping when
> I lay my burdens down."

CARLYLE STEWART

Age: 87
622 Columbus Street, McDonoghville, Louisiana
Interviewer: Flossie McElwee
May 3, 1940

"My master name wuz Octave De la Houssaye. I wuz borned in 1853, the third day of January, at Jeanerette [just south of Lafayette in Iberia Parish]. I was seven years old but didn't do my master much good when we wuz sat [*sic*] free. My maw brung us here in a flat car and went to the Touro building, my mother was a seamster.

"When the Yankees came they put her in the fields and she left home after the freedom came. They came on horses (The Calavary [*sic*] on horses you know), and they liked to have scared me to deth [*sic*] with their swords slanking [clanking]. The boss (My Marse) was good to us, but when we was freed, one of the bosses kicked my ma in the face. I was only seven but I 'member when Mr. Alfred kicked my maw and make a big lump on her face. I worked, carr'ing sugarcane, I could only tote five stalks at a time.

"The old slave driver uncle Ned dey axed him where was the Rebs and he pointed and said that way—and the bosses grabbed him and threw him in the river. They were the Rebs, themselves. He shouda stayed in and left his mouf shut, my old God-mother and God-father, we wuz all posted to stay in and be quite [quiet], and he was so smart, he went out and they fixed him.

"We had no pleasure at all and when they went to beat us women, they dug a hole and put the women's stom'ch in the hole, when she was pregnant, so they could whip them without having the child hurt, cause the children were worth money.

"After I come here, I worked for Mrs. Julia Behrman, Mr. Stanley's mother. I stayed 9 yrs. I worked for Deckers 20 yrs. and raised their children, and for Mrs. Lohman, I worked 40 yrs. for her. Her sons are all old and grey headed like me.

"Oh Yes! They had straps and a whip and they'd better not catch you praying to God. When you prayed you had to hide in the woods.

"We had grits and cornmeal and sometimes side meat and 'lasses. Not often we had meat, tho, we raised it on the place.

"My mother's name was Jane Geambo and father's surname was Johnson Jean Pierre Geambo, a Guinea Nigger. They brought my grandpa from Afficay. He was an Afficun Nigger. They stole him from there and my mother was born in New Iberia.

"We didn't have no shoes and I wore a cottonade gown made of this blue denim. We didn't know what 'draws' [underwear] wuz. You couldn't say your prayer let 'lone read and write. I knowed my prayers. My mother teached me behind the Marse's back in her old dark house. She made candle with beef tallow. And we didn't suffer from cold when we got in our bed with my maw and her five chellin—then we wuz warm. . . .

"When I married down the coast, dey just take a piece of paper and read the matrimony to us.

"But all my papers and my aunt's wedding ring floated off in a truck. When the high waters came, the first high water—we were in three high waters down the coast.

"They christined [*sic*] me in Catholic church at St. Patout. The church is still there and my age too. I had seven chillums. Thank God they never had slaves when dey were brung up!

"My step-pa was sold when he wuz 12 yrs. old. He ain't never seed his maw again.

"I was just Catholic and pray in my house at nite. I never got that 'legion [religion] that makes you shout and carry on."

BATON ROUGE AREA

Cutting cane into carts in Plaquemines Parish
Courtesy of the State Library of Louisiana

CATHERINE CORNELIUS

Age: 103
Lafon Old Folks' Home, 3501 South Robertson Street
Interviewer: Breaux McKinney
[The Lafon Home has continually operated in New
Orleans since 1842 by the Sisters of the Holy Family. It
was named after its benefactor the philanthropist Thomy
Lafon, a free man of color.]

Mrs. Catherine Cornelius, an ex-slave who is reputed
to be 103 years old, [was] "born in a log cabin" in Smithfield, a large plantation in west Louisiana. She said that the
location of the plantation would now be about twelve miles
above Baton Rouge. [Note: This is not west Louisiana.]

Catherine is an inmate of the Lafon Old Folks' Home,
(Protestant) 3501 S. Robertson St. She is comely and sur-
prisingly energetic, dark complexioned and weighs about
ninety pounds. She wore a black dress with a blue and white
dotted apron tied around her waist, black tignon with slippers to match. The only apparent infirmaty [*sic*] from which
she suffers is a slight deafness, this being due to her age.
For a person as advanced in years, Mrs. Cornelius has an

unusually keen mind. She has apparently had a quiet and sane life, and strange to say, not in the least superstitious, having no belief in voodoo, not even being familiar with the name of Marie Laveau.

The interview which, due to the cold weather, was held in the dining room is as follows:

"Ah was a slave an raised on de Smithfield plantation an came to N'Awlins in de surrender of Abe Lincoln an bin hyar ever since. Lawd, Ah was a grown woman when dat war broke out. Ah wurked in de field cuttin cane. Ma ma and pa an de whole family was dere too. Ma ma an pa came from Richmond, Virginia. Ma ma worked in de field an my ma was a lady's maid. Dere names was Frederick and Nancy Brown. Ah kin still remember mah ma's funeral. Dey sho gave her a nice funeral. All of de slaves on de plantation had a nice funeral. De preacher on de place, Brudder Aaron, wurked on de plantation cuttin' cane[. W]henever dey had any services fo him to make dey jus call him out of de field. De slaves burial grounds was a gud place back of de plantations. No, we [had] no markers or head stones but we planted willow trees to knoe [*sic*] de place whar one of yo kins was buried. Dey jus used wooden boxes fo coffins an dey was made by de carpenters on de place. De bodies was carried in carts an de odders walked. Whenever anybody died dey all was let off from work to go to the funeral. De hymn dey sang fo mah mother's funeral went lak dis:

> Back from de doleful sound
> Mah ears intend to cry
> De livin' men come view de ground

Prince say de clay must be ya bed
Inspite [*sic*] of all ya toils
De clay must be ya bed.

Reverend Heywood who is in charge of the home was in the room when Catherine sang the hymn. He very obligingly got an old hymn book which he said "is well over a hundred years old." The hymn she sang [credited to Isaac Watts] was in it. . . .

A Voice from the Tombs

Hark! From the tombs a doleful sound;
My ears, attend the cry:
Ye living men, come view the ground where you
    must shortly lie.

"Princes, this clay must be your bed,
In spite of all your towers;
The tall, the wise, the reverend head, must be as
    low as ours."

Great God! Is this our certain doom?
And are we still secure?
Still walking down to the tomb, and yet prepared
    no more?

Grant us the power of quickening grace,
To fit our souls to fly;
Then when we drop this dying flesh, we'll rise
    above the sky.

"De plantation sat on de ribber. Dere was mo den a hundred slaves on it. De cabins was white an dere was one family to a cabin. What did dey [do] fo us when we was sick? Why, we had a nice hospital in de place with a Negro nurse an mid-wife. An not only Doctor Lyles but a doctor from town tended us. Doctor Lyles would call us an give us money on Christmas an holidays an when de showboats would cum to town. He'd giv us fifty cents. Shucks, we didn't need no money in dem days. We got everything we wanted to eat. We had plenty of clothes to wear. We had everything de white folks had, all de meat an vegetables we wanted. Dey gav us de goods, cottonade, that was made on de place an we made our clothes. De shoes was heavy work shoes an dey was made on de place too. We had Saturday an Sunday off but we had to go to church. Saturday was de day we did our washing, sewin and cleaning up de house. Dat was de day fo ourselves. We all had certain tasks to do. If we finished dem ahead of time de rest of de day was ours. Christmas week we had a week's holiday. Sho we had gud times. We had singin, dancin an visitin among ourselves an on udder plantations.

"We had big times. Ah was named after mah young Mistress, Miss Catherine. All of de slaves was christened in de church. We nebher had no ribber baptism on our place. De church in town dat we went to was called de Episcopalian church. We had no special days to git married. We jest said dat we wanted to git married an Doctor Lyles married us. Yeah, we had a little celebration among us. We had sweet cakes an a little frolic. No, de people from de big house didn't come down to our cabins an our celebrations. Dey would come down sometimes to see us but on no special day. No, we didn't have no schools on de plantation.

"Doctor Lyles was de son-in-law of Mrs. Smith who had anudder plantation in Bayou Sara [a historical port near St. Francisville]. She raised cotton. On our plantation we raised mostly cotton, sugar and corn. We had a sugar house right on de plantation. If we was bad dey would whip us an put us in stocks but we nebber had no trouble on our plantation. You know it was a big plantation cause Ah remember well [the] dey [day] Ah was standin on de levee when [Union] General [Benjamin] Butler was on his way to the siege of Vicksburg. He said 'Girls, what town is dis?' Ah said, 'Dis aint no town, dis a plantation.' Dey camped de furst night, de soldiers slept under de bell. De nex' day dey went up de ribber. Lawd, when dey came Ah didn't know what dat was comin up de ribber. Ah knew it wasn't no house or showboat but Ah didn't think it was a war boat, cos Ah had nebber seen one.

"Mah master put up a white flag but dem Yankees tore it down. De missus was in Turnbull an was askin dat dey send her niggers to her. Dey took us to Bayou Sara to hide us in tents on de plantation dere but de Yankees found us. Mah boss had horses as fast as lightnin. Dey would fly jus lik black buzzards. Ah remember well. Mah boss was in his buggy when de Yankees came. When he saw dem he started to run from his buggy, but fell. De doctor went to him but he said, 'Dis man is dead.' De Yankees took loads of money dat mah missus an master had. It was carried in iron safes. De Yankees took all dere money to Port Hudson in som kind of wagon. Ah was right in de middle of de war. Ah hyar [heard] de guns and de bullets. Dey went lak dis 'pop, pop, pop, pop.' De Yankees gav us money. It was de first time dat Ah had seen Yankee money. Ah didn't know what to de [*sic*] with dat Yankee money. Ah lef mines in de stomp of a tree but Ah sho wish dat Ah had it now. De Yankees brought us hyar [here] in a boat. We wus first to de old barracks, dats de furst place dey took us. Mah furst husband was Wylie Smith. He wurked in de field. Ah bin married agin a second time an got a daughter but Ah don know whar she is. Mah brother, Beverly Brown, died in de war. Ah nebber want to see anudder war."

Note: Because Mrs. Cornelius was becoming fatigued we ended the interview and promised to call again.

JOHN MCDONALD

Age: unknown
Essen Lane Road, Baton Rouge, Louisiana
Interviewer: Tatum

"No suh, boss I can't read and write. When I were brung up ef'n my boss man kotch me wit a pencil or paper it was 25 lashes.

"Yes, suh, we had plenty dem old time cures. You know de doctor give us quinine and bitters, but we used plenty 'assfetida' [asafetida] and rabbit foots to hope [help] out. We'd tie a bit of 'assfetida' up in a rag and put it round the babies neck to keep colds away and to hope it when dey cuts teeth. Then a bone from a possum's tail makes em break the tooth fru the gum on time. I always keep a rabbit foot and a buckeye in my pocket to keep rumatizm off. Never plant peas, beans, etc., in the full moon. Plant taters and goobers then.

"Have your cows come fresh in the spring and they'll give more milk. If you want to keep a cow milking a long time never let the calf touch her bag, just keep it milked out for several days and as soon as the milk gets strong enough start milking every morning and night reglar [*sic*]. Never milk a cow's milk on the ground, as it will make her go dry.

"Witches? No suh I aint never had no truck wid none, but I'se seed sperits.

"We had a old sow what had a sperit in her. She'd take de sperit every time she had a litter er pirgs [pigs], and wont nobody go near her den. I member de time she put me atop a stump in de barn yard and mind me dere all night. Just de sperit o' de devil in her, that's what. Soon as day break came she goes on arbout [*sic*] her business peaceful like as could be. Folks say when a body dies wid things on dere mind dere sperit goes in a dog, or hog or any animal near by. The sperit in this animal then acts on the thing in folks mind when they die. If you don't hab no worries on you mind when you dies the sperit rests. I'se seen rabbits with sperits what ain't act no way natchrel. Neber seed no ghosts, but I ain't zactly look for none.

"Cure for measles? Well, now, dere aint none. Just keep your hands off dem pison [*sic*] bushes and be careful to stay in doors. They ain't gonna hurt you none if'n you keep a rabbit foot handy bout your person."

ALBERT PATTERSON

Age: 90
2224 Freret Street [New Orleans]
Interviewer: Maud Wallace
May 22, 1940

2224 Freret St. is one of those typical New Orleans double houses. From the front door with green blinds, the shutters closed, there are three steps down to the sidewalk, scoured immaculately clean, and here, on the top step, in the shade of a china-ball tree growing at the edge of the sidewalk, is seated an old, thin, light-tan negro. He is Albert Patterson. Dressed in dark trousers, a white shirt, open at the neck, a dark straw hat and holding a cane. He is leaning against the door, and looks as clean as the steps, and as cool as the shade of the china-ball tree. He lives in one room in the back of the house.

"An' I gits along fine. The Welfare give me five-fifty every two weeks. That takes care o' me. I got two children livin' but I never hear from them. My boy's in Texas, my girl's in Chicago. A lady here in de block had a daughter what go to Chicago jes' a few weeks ago, an' when she come back she say my daughter's livin' in de same address what I write to her, but she won' answer my letters, because she don' want the niggers up there to know she was born in de South.

"I was borned in eighteen-fifty, on a place called Lasco Plantation, Plaequimine [Plaquemines] Parish. It was afterwards called Junior Plantation, an' I lived in de South all my life.

"We raised sugar cane an' made sugar, no refinery, we'd boil it in big kittles [*sic*] an' there was a colored man from Mississippi that know when the sugar grain. We'd work in fields in de day an' make sugar at night.

"We had no schools, they wouldn't let a nigger look at a school.

"Colonel White built us a church, a Baptist Church, an' we had it way after de war. We had no pleasures, jes' work, only on the fourth o' July, they kill a beef an' have a big barbecue.

"There was regular quarters fo' de colored people an' a big cook house, a woman cooked fo' dem while dey worked.

"I remember our plantation was sold twice befo' de war. It was sheriff's sale, de white peoples dey stand up on de porch, an' de black men an' women an' children stand on de ground an' de man he shout, 'How much am I offered fo' plantation an' fine men an' women?' Somebody would say so many thousand an' de man would yell 'Look at dem little niggers, dey's worth so many thousand a year.' An' after while, one man buy it all. If a nigger come from de north with a trade, he sold for six thousand dollars, but de man that buys him gets ten dollars a day fo' his work. [Slaves skilled in carpentry or brick masonry brought high prices,

since they could be rented out to other plantation owners.]
It's jes' like pullin' a leaf out o' that tree.

"My father was sold up in Ascension Parish to a bad man, but he wouldn't work. De man learned him a trade, an' then he ran away to come back an' see his family, he ran away seventy-five miles. He got on a flat boat in Natchez, an' was three months driftin' down to the coast, but he wouldn't plow or hoe, an' de overseer couldn't hit him 'cause Col. White wouldn't allow that, he was a good man.

"De Frenchmen an' de Dutchmen were mean, but the Irishmen was good. I seen de blood cut out o' niggers dat deep, seen it wid my own eyes, but not Col. White. He not cruel, he wouldn't whip, he'd punish. He had a iron band, he'd rivet to go around the ankle, an' he had a iron band to go around the neck with a piece o' iron standin' up in de front, de back an' each side[. Y]o' had to hold yo' head jes' so, an' yo' couldn't lay down, an' yo' had to pad that iron band, 'cause it was so heavy it would cut yo' neck, but he never kept no nigger dogs, an' he had a great big woods in de back where de niggers would hide when they run away, but he wouldn't let nobody bring nigger dogs to find them. If a nigger hide in de woods, he'd come in at night, an' to get [a] meal. They bore a little hole in the floor an' they break into de meat house too. De dogs couldn't catch dem nohow, 'cause they put Bay Leaves on de bottom o' their feet an' shoes, then they go an' walk in fresh manure an' a dog can't track them. That way a man could come an' see his family, an' when it's time to get busy to gather crops they'd come out o' the woods, walk up to Col. White, an' say 'I'll take de crops off if'n yo'll let me.'

"I remember when de gunboats come up de river an'

took Jackson an' St. Phillips Fort an' [Union] General [Benjamin] Butler took New Orleans. I seen some bad things. I seen de Rebel soldiers run, wid their leg most cut off to de knee, or de arm hangin', de blood pourin'. De Colonel, he make me carry dem in de buggy, so they could come here to de hospital, an' then some o' them start cussin', an' insist they goin' right back to de battlefield even with their arm cut off so they can't carry a gun.

"I remember there was one man, a big hard man, a overseer—he was a great speech maker. He used to make speeches to make the men go an' fight an' if they didn't go, he'd jump on them an' beat them, even his own brother an' his own son—an' he lost them. He made every man go fight what he could, but he never did go. One boy, he say he walk five miles through a battlefield lookin' fo' his father. He never find him, but say men there full o' blood, hundreds o' them on de ground an' beggin' him to kill them; but the war today more crueler than it was then. 'Course through de war then, we couldn't buy salt, but back in those days we had more food than we got now, always plenty pickled beef an' molasses. When de government took de plantations, they started paying wages. The Yankees didn't bother Col. White. He put up a big United States Flag right in front of his house an' he used to make a lot o' wine, so the Yankees thought that fine.

"'There was a white man, a overseer, Joe Bates an' his driver Edward Jackson. He was on de Oak Point Plantation. Since freedom, he was havin' trouble wid de bank, so he drive all night an' come to de city to Marie Leveau's because he use to pay her to keep his job fo' him, but when he get here to her, she say, 'Yo' one hour too late[. Y]o' belongin's is already on de river front.' An' when he git back to Oak Point, there was all his things on de river front. I didn't never see her, but this white man Joe Bates, he tell it hisself that he jes' a hour too late gettin' to Marie Leveau.

"I never know much about de hoodoo, but de spirits yes! I seen dem an' they don' do no harm. God is spirit ain't He?

"Years ago I got into my bed one night an' de cover it pull off. I didn't think much about it, an' pulled it up again, but the third time it pulled off, I got on my knees an' say my prayers an' de covers don' pull off no more. Then about twenty years ago, I went to de Charity Hospital with de pneumonia an' I was already seventy, but de first time I ever sick. There was a little short yellow [mulatto] in de bed next to me an' I don't know him at all, but he die. Well that night he come to my bed, an' he try to put his hands on me, he laugh an' say, I'm goin' with him, but I slip out o' de bed on de other side an' I git on my knees an' I pray, an' I'm still here. Yo' see my mother she had six children, I'm de first an' de others are all gone, so I'm de first an' de last."

ROBERT ST. ANN

Age: 95
3521 Gibson Street, New Orleans, Louisiana
First Interview
Interviewer: Maud Wallace

"Cousin Bob," as he is known to everyone . . . , was seated in the rocking chair on the front porch. He is a black Negro with white hair, looks strong and healthy, although he is quite old.

"I was borned August tenth, eighteen forty-four, in Plaqumine [Plaquemines Parish], called Gueno Settlement. It was a fine place, ten acres front on de river, back to de swamp.

"Dey was jes' five slaves; it was a rice farm an' orange grove; course dey raised everything we eat too; dey was jes' de two families, each had dey own single house; dere was no school an' de church must a been forty or fifty miles away.

"We had a good master, he never beat any o' us, he say 'my slave's human, like me.'

"De chillun use to play an' yo' do de work yo' ole enough to do.

"De rice fields sho' is pretty, first dey is all green, den all white blossoms, den when dey fall it starts bendin' over an' it gets yaller; if it gets too tall a strong wind blow it down. In de ole slave days, we use to cut wid sickle an' cradle, den tie it in bundles to dry, dat was de best rice too, we'd cut like Thursday an' hull it Saturday. Yo' works den on a plantation, dat's work dat has to be done right now! We starts cuttin' first o' August. To thrash it, we used to put a post in de ground about four feet deep, den we'd pack it an' stomp it 'cause it had to be hard ground. Den we'd hitch de horses two a-bref [abreast] to de post; we puts de rice on de ground, de horses keep circlin' as fast as dey can. Yo' put a fast one on de outside an' de ole one next to de post, an' yo' keeps turnin' de rice an' de horse keeps trompin' on it; den yo' cleans all de dirt out, keep fanin' [sic] de rice till its clean, den yo' puts it in bags, we gets fifty to seventy-five barrels in a day.

"Yo' up befo' daybreak an' yo' work hard wid de crop till yo' gits through, 'cause de crop won't wait on yo'.

"Some o' de pore black people though[t] dey had it hard. Yo'll excuse me fo' tellin' yo' dis, but I seen 'em take a woman what was prejudice [pregnant] an' dey make a hole big enough fo' her to put her stomache [sic] in, dey raise her clothes, an' beat her wid a strap till de blood come, den dey pour brine over her.

"I remembers once a youngster run away an' dey put de blood hounds behind him, when dey caught him, dey put a horse to him an' drag him through de woods, drag him to de house, de bref [breath] plum out o' him. Dey dig a hole an' throw him in it an' after, yo' hear dat boy grown [groan] under de ground, he ain't daid.

"Ole man Grun he put a woman's eye out wid a fork, jes' stuck it in her eye like dat an' pull it. An' he takes men [and] hitch dem to de plows, make dem pull like de mules.

"If de patrols catch a slave in de road, he beat them, 'cause he ain't supposed to be out at night.

"Dere was Thompson West, what never worked a day from de time dey took him from de trades yard, dat's de place in de city where dey sell de slaves an' de people come from de country, buy dem an' take dem back. Thompson, he hide in de woods, I dunno how he live, but when de Yankees come, he walk out an' say 'I'm a free man.'

"De Yankees start to bombard through Jackson an' Ft. St. Phillip[.] De Confederates was lookin' fo' dem to come up de river an' dey put up chains, but back o' de place dey call de Jump [unknown] dey started throwin' bullets like rain. At night it looked like hundreds o' fire crackers all lit up[. D]ey started at Thursday evein' [*sic*] an' Friday at five A.M. de fort was empty, an' here come de Yankees, some blacks wid 'em, right on through.

"Dey knew the good masters an' never hurt dem, but ask me what dey treat those mean ones?

"There was one man what called all his slaves to him an' asked the Yankees not to hurt dem, but de slaves say dey not goin' nowhere[,] dey gonna stay right there with their master an' de Yankees couldn't make dem move.

"Then ole man Poilet he had a man named Jim. His overseer whip him in de fiel' an' Jim take his cane knife an' cut him. That night the men come an' say 'Jim gotta be whipped by de law.' But ole man Poilet he say 'anybody whip dis ole nigger'—excuse me de way I tell it, but he slap right here, where yo' set—'it's gonna be me. I bought him an' paid fo' him an' I don' believe in beatin'.' An' Jim, stand right there by his master an' nobody touch him.

"Some had it hard an' some had it easy. I worked on different farms about sixteen years, till de rice got so low.

"When I come here, I work in de sugar refinery, in de sewerage, an' on de water front. I work till nineteen thirty-one, den dey say I'm too ole an' dey won't let me work, but dey won't give me nothin' to do. The society let me sleep here an' my friends, they feed me when they can.

"I work a long time on a boat called the *F. and J.* fo' Captain Freddy Vanderbrooke. He use to carry freight an' oysters. We carry nine hundred sacks oysters. In the storm, September 1915 we were out, an' I never forget, that boat sink in shallow water an' we all go upstairs, all at once Captain Freddy, he call 'look out, cabin goin' off!' an' it did, into de water we went[. W]e fit [fought] the water an' fit it an' when we was picked up, we had gone seventeen miles. They bring us back by train; the news had got out we drowned, but Captain Freddy, he tell dem 'the boat, he drown but no lives.' I come on home an' my wife an' chillun cry; she say, 'Papa, how yo' make out' but I cain't tell her.

"Then Captain Freddy make up his mind to get the Hull[. A] lot o' his white friends an' he take me, go with him, but she was thirteen hundred feet out in de prairie—no water, hard dry land, so he comes, gets a cable, we pull, but it breaks. His friends, one by one leave him, an' jes' me an' Captain Freddy left. I spliced that cable an' we made a pull, she made her nose to the water. I tole him if I get that wench out, I'm gonna get drunk. Sho' enongh [*sic*] when we got her out, he get whiskey an' beer. Mamma had food, so I set down to it.

"After the boat rebuilt, Captain Freddy he say 'de law on dis boat is, yo' vacant place shall never be filled,' an' I stay there till Captain Freddy died. When I got too old he made me watchman, he could trust me, I never touch his money or whiskey, but I sure did like his candy.

"Oh yes, Marie Leveau, I never see her, but I hear people say terrible things about her. When she die she tell them to look under a doorstep an' they find a little baby she kilt. Then dey put two horses to her hearse, an' dey pull but dey cain't move her, dey put two more horses an dey pull an' dey strain, dey rared upon their hind laigs but dey couldn't move her.

"I don't know how dey got that woman buried, but I know one thing—I sure hope they did."

Second Interview
Interviewer: Michinard
August 1940

Coz. Bob, as he is known, was born on August 10, 1848 [note discrepancy versus first interview], he was a slave of Mr. Guillot Chartier, in Plaquemines.

"My master was good at times, for [before] he drank hard," he says.

"My Mars had four sons and three daughters, one of them was my godmother. I was christened in St. Thomas' Catholic Church in Point-a-la Hache by Father Savilie, who was killed by 18 men who came together, each one in turn stabbed him."

The Church was built on a hill, in the valley was a large settlement of Indians. I asked Bob if he mingled with the Indians. He said,

"No sar, I was too scared of them. When they come to talking their language and begin making their motions I'se was terrified. My ma she used to say: '*Cha pas besoin avoir peur ca c'est du monde comme toi.*' Meaning: You need not be scared[,] them are peoples like you."

Coz. Bob is very proud to say that he was never arrested in his life.

Bob remembers when the Yankees bombarded Fort St. Philip and Fort Jackson. He says it was on a Thursday and on Friday, about four A.M., the Confederates ran away. Bob says it was a pitiful sight to see the poor Confederate soldiers, as they passed his master's place. They were without shirts, without shoes, and bare headed.

SHACK WILSON

Age: unknown
2926½ First Street
Interviewer: Miss Z. Posey

"We're marching home day by day, marching to the beautiful lan' of God."

In response to our request for some "way-back-yonder" songs, this old Negro who says he is trying to forget all those horrible days of slavery, sings these lines which were used in the field while coaxing the mules along and adds:

"Way back yonder I was born in Clinton, La. [in East Feliciana Parish], and belonged to Marse D. Robbins. Lor' I remember when I had a pair of pants made out of Lowell cloth and I felt so dressed up and proud. That was after slavery and we didn't have much money.

"Lowell cloth? Why, it's a heavy cotton stuff and it's white and it's most everlasting. My Pa was a slave ox-driver and once when he went to head off some oxen he shagged his leg and he died of it.

"They used to whip slaves if they didn't pick enough cotton. They put four pegs in the ground and tied one leg to one peg, the other to the other and the arms were tied together. They were stripped of all clothing and whipped with a raw hide.

" 'Do pray, Marster, Do pray, Marster, Hi-yi-Hi-yi' until their cries almost died away. Then they'd put to picking cotton with all that suffering, and, if a slave run away, they'd put a pack of 'nigger dogs' on their trail. Some people call them bloodhounds, but they uster to [*sic*] be called nigger dogs.

"Niggers always loved to sing, but it wasn't in slavery that we did much of it. One thing was we didn't have a mind on it, even if we had been 'lowed, an' it night when we went to our house, we was too tired an' sleepy, but after freedom, Lor' how we did sing! We sang when we went to Church and when we were at work and all the time it seems like. We worked 'taters, sweet 'taters," an' then he broke out with:

> Grasshopper settin' on sweet 'tater vine,
> Ole turkey-gobbler come struttin' up behin',
> Snipped Grasshopper off sweet 'tater vine.

"We were called lazy an' it seem lak we never could get enuf sleep. So lots o' times 'specially in warm weather, we jes' natchuly dozed, an' then we'd hear mebbe, that ol' fiel' lark a singin':

> Laziness'll kill you,
> Laziness'll kill you.

" 'Twas all right for that ol' bird to repriman' us if he hadn't been havin' the easiest life of anythin'.

"Birds got lots of sense—more'n some people. That ol' Shiverin' owl, sometimes called the death-bird, knows just when somebody will die and where.

"We uster sing:

> Of all the varmints in the woods,
> I'd rather be a coon,
> An' carry my tail curled up my bac',
> An' get up in the mornin' soon!

"It's gettin' pretty close to the time when all the cows fall on their knees in reverence to God who was born at 12 o'clock on Christmas. At this time they all do it, jus' watch 'em an' see.

"An' they say chickens crow more near Christmas than any other time, it's because they're rejoicin'.

"If you want to know what the weather is going to be, watch the moon. If both the horns or points are upwards, the weather will be dry, if sideways or down—it will be rainy. If it's round like it could hold water, the weather will be dry but if it's downward, like it can't hold water, look out for rain or wet weather.

"In old times we took May pops, they grow on a vine an' are a pretty red, they are nice and juicy to suck and when they yellow an' dry, we put 'em in our pockets for scent when we went to Church an' parties.

"Simmon [persimmon] bread we made an' it was good an' 'tater bread, too. . . .

"I never went in for conjure. It's the work of Ol' Satan. Way back yonder, some of these people took cat an' 'possum tails an' tied 'em with a string of red flannel an' carried them in their pockets to do somethin'—I forgotten what.

"My ma used to sing:

> Got my 'ligion [religion] in hard time,
> Jesus giv' her a legal ring,
> O, may we go, I'm on the way,
> Stay, Marster, stay an' tell my Jesus,
> I'm on the way.

"In the old times, we were our own druggis' an' doctor an' cured ourself with roots an' herbs an' home-made remedies.

"Collard leaves we put on head for misery, an' again we made a poultice with them for biles [boils]. Once, when I had a carbuckle [carbuncle] on the back of my neck an' they said I was goin' to die, I cured myself with it.

"When we wanted to stop bleedin' we got a han'ful of soot outer the chim'ly [chimney] an' it would quit. Cobwebs did the same thin'. If you got a sprain take clay[,] mix it with vinegar, bind it on the wrench an' it goes out.

"When chil'ren had worms their mammy made a tea of Jerusaley [Jerusalem] weed an' it was a wormifuge that cured 'em.

"When palate was down all you had to do was to lif' up a tuff of hair from top of head an' tie it with a cord an' in three days it was all right.

"They didn't bleed much in my time, but when I heered say when they thought a person had too much blood an' it was dangerous, they sent for a doctor an' he would come an' bleed them but they don't do that anymo'[. N]ow it seems lak they mus' put blood in you.

"My Pa an' Ma used to tell of the brutal treatment of their ol' Marster. T'want he that was so mean, but that ol' overseer. No wonder she used to sing:

> Before I'd be a slave,
> I'd be ded in my grave,
> An' go home to my Father,
> An' be saved.

"Nigger had no use for white folks that had riz [risen in status] or were common. We uster say: 'I'd rather be a nigger than pore white trash.' But everybody wasn't hard[.] Some were good an' kind; in my town, Clinton, where I wuz born an' raised, there was a lady named Silliman an' ev'rybody liked her. Once she fell down an' broke her collar-bone an' died. In her will she left ground to some ol' servants, some had been slaves. Jim Monroe got 200 acres, Dorothy Speer, 75, Borey Hare an' Willie Hare, 75 each, Dee Matthews, 75, Chester Cannon, 75, an' to another, 75. She wanted to give them a start in life."

"Was Silliman College named for this lady?" we asked.

"Yes'm, it wuz, for her an' her husban' an' it's one of the prettiest places you ever did see. Nice ol' live oaks all 'round. It sho' am fine.

"An' you've heered of Mrs. Silliman? I'm glad because you know that what I say is true. Some folks say nigger is all imagination. Ain't it funny how things turn 'round? When I wuz little, we liked peanuts, only we didn't give that name. We called 'em 'hog-peas' and nobody hardly but niggers ate them, now they're considered good and sell on the streets, jas' a little bag for a nickel. People useter get 'em in a gunny-sack for feed, that is those that didn't raide 'em."

And then we expatriated upon their qualities, medicinally, gastronomically, commercially. How physicians were prescribing them for their nervous patients. But they must be eaten raw—another instance of going back to nature. Even the hulls are not wasted for they are used as a fertilizer. But peanuts, goobers, ground-peas or fainders, just whichever state dubs them, they are good to eat!

"And we uster hair [sic] all the 'coons an' 'possums us could eat. 'Possums are the bes'. Beavers are bes' of any but they were not so easy to ketch, besides they were so sly; now I jes' don' believe they is ennymo'. But the beaver sho' is fine tender meat. Did you ever see 'em at work? Well, I reckon not—'cause they scampede [sic] when anyone comes near, but you can look at the wreck they made!

"They eat the bark off trees an' the leaves an' the roots and berries. They mos'ly live about the river an' bayous where they have lots of trees an' plants. My, how they can destroy trees, big ones, sometimes. Two or three work to cut the bark all 'roun' and they keep at it until the tree topples over. This makes a sort of bridge to cross to [the] other side, then they pile up mud an' it dries with the tree, then they pound it down with their tails, they got power in those tails!

"They build houses out of mud to stay in when it's too col' to be out. We sol' the skins to make hats for men outen. Tall, shiny hats."

"Yes, and you used 'coon skins, too, did you not?"

"Yes, man, we sho' did. We made 'em ourselves, an' we let the tail hang down in the bac'."

Coon skin and beaver skins both used as a covering for the head, one for the lowly son of toil, the other as a hall-mark of gentility!

In Louisiana, where embankments were weak, beavers were of inestimable value in preparing marsh drainage.

But negroes would kill and eat them.

The story is told of a planter who, on discovering this slaughter harshly threatens his negroes. Instead of being struck dumb with shame one of them replied:

"We poor fellows spend all our time in praying for others and have no one to pray for ourselves. [N]o wonder we fall into temptation."

We repeated this story to the old negro, who seemed much impressed with it. "That's a fac'. It sholy [surely] is, but we can always pray: 'Lead us not into tem'tation,' an' if we follow He's [sic] Will, an' Commandments it ain't so hard."

On the wall of the general room in which Shack Wilson lives, hangs a framed, marriage license. As you look at it you are impressed that in this man is a man of honor and integrity who follows as best he can, the footsteps of His meek and lowly Master.

"Yes'm, come lak that paper say, April 25 nex' I was married years ago, an' when she died I been true to her mem'ry."

Jean Étienne de Boré (1740–1820) introduced the sugar crystallization process to Louisiana in the 1790s, thus triggering the growth of sugar cane as a commercial crop. In 1803, he became the first mayor of New Orleans.
Courtesy of State Library of Louisiana

PETER BARBER

Age: 96
Lafon Old Folks Home of the Holy Family Convent
New Orleans, Louisiana
Interviewer: Burke
August 23, 1940

Peter Barber is an inmate of the Lafon Old Folks Home. He claims to be one hundred and six years old, but according to the dates he remembers quite well, he is only 96. Peter Barber is about six feet tall and at this age weighs one hundred seventy pounds and is well proportioned. His dark skin makes a distinct contrast with his gray hair, gray beard, and his bushy beetle gray eyebrows, under which deepset [*sic*] eyes require no glasses. He is well preserved and remarkably active, a fact in which he prides himself. He also prides himself in talking, giving a creditable demonstration as he sketched the highlights of a rather eventful life.

"Young man, I'm always glad to talk about the life that I've lived, and because of it I am not ashamed. But the first thing I wanter tell you is that I was a slave. And it is said that 'one brother *shouldn't* hold another one a slave.' Did you hear me? He said shouldn't but they did right on. And they musta thought they was right and if I hadn't been a slave up until the time I was a young man, I might not be here today.

"I was born in Charlottesville, Virginia, and I can remember from the time I was eight years old. My first master was named William Granger. He was a farmer. He owned a large farm and he owned a saw mill and a grist mill. My mistress was the one who taught me how to write, and every year she would make us, all the slaves, write our ages in a big Bible she had just for that purpose. 'Course you see that's the way she kep' a record of all of us.

"My master was good too, but he didn't take no pains with us. As long as we worked he didn't bother. But he treated us well. Clo'es, food, and a place to stay in and no bad hard words.

"I grew to be a big, strong boy and I could do my work well. And I don't know why we was sold to our second master—Sam Austin. He was tobacco man. They sold me for $900—half Confederate and half Union money. When I was with Austin I was the foreman up to the time [Union general Ulysses S.] Grant took Richmond. Then, he tried to fool us. He said, 'I'm gonner send y'all up to the Blueridge [*sic*] Mountains, on account of they's gonner wanner capture ya, them Yankees.' Well, I had been kinder looking inter the things all the while and I knowed jes what they had been fightin for. And for everyone that knowed, there was ten thousand that didn't know. But I kep' my mouth and head and didn't say nuthin, but I went and my buddie, his name was Jimm[i]e Harris[,] and I told him I thought we should run away. So we did. We stored [*sic*] away on the Ohio and Chesapeake. I was twenty-two when we ran away. That's why I kin say I knowed what slavery was. Cause I was old enough to know what it was all about. I worked in the fields and in tobacco sheds. I got it first hand, not by somebody telling me. So when our master talked about sending us up in the mountains, I knew better.

"Well, anyway, we was headin for Cincinatti [*sic*], Ohio but we didn't quite git there. So we stopped by a river and somebody told us that a boat was comin along. I had never seen a boat in my life and I got anxious to see it. So we waited. But she didn't come. It got dark and the boys dug in at the landing and ate their supper, but shucks, I didn't want nuthin to eat. I had never seen a boat. A long time afterwards, I looked down the river and saw a red light and a green light. Then when she came closer I could see the black smoke jes purin [pouring] outer her stacks. I jes stood there and looked. And when I looked and saw the people on it and the mule teams and the wagons and everything else, I had ter wonder 'cause here I was: if I'd jes so much as step in that river why I'd sink and here was something big as a house and it was floatin.

"While they was loadin up me and my partner got on and when she didn't tilt over when that big mule team left, I said I guessed it was all right. That boat was the *C. P. Hanni-can* and she was headed for Cincinatti [*sic*] jes where we was goin, but the next day somebody asked us if we was deck hands. Not thinkin we said no. Well, they knowed we wasn't passengers, so they said, 'We're gonner put you off at the nex landing.' And it was a tough lil town they put us off in, but we didn't stay there too long. After gittin a glimpse of it and seein what a tough place it was we kep on goin and we walked the rest of the way.

"We got in Cincinatti [*sic*] and you know we didn't know nuthin about fast life and dressin up like the other fellers we saw, so we kinder shied away from the other folks. On this account we saved our money. We had about two or three hundred dollars apiece and very little of it did we spend.

"After lookin around for a while me and Jimm[i]e, that's my buddie, we went to join up with the Army. So they examined Jimm[i]e first and he passed the test. An he was outfitted. Then the officer looker [*sic*] at me. Then he says, 'You wanter join the Army too?' I told him yes, sir, and he looked at me agin, sizing me up and he took so long until I started to feelin funny. After a while he looked at the other officer an said, 'We'll take him in—about two more years.' I liketa cried. How in the world could they take Jimm[i]e Harris and not take me? For the life of me I could never understand. But to this day I tell ya it's the one thing that saved my life. I'll tell ya about that a little later. But ya know Jimmie was proud of his suit and everybody was hollering at him and wishin him good luck. 'Course you know how I felt an specially when they started ta askin me where was my suit.

"But I jes laughted [*sic*] kinder sickly like and said I wasn't ready to join up yit. So, I want to work and got me a job on a boat. I don know but look like to me, ever since I seen the *C. P. Hannican* and rid on her, looks like to me I had a hankerin to travel on the water and I worked up and down on the Ohio River on the *C. B. Church* which was runnin in outer Cincinatti [*sic*] at the time. I was gittin mostly broke in but I was learnin fast and in two, three years I was a first class deck hand.

"Long about that time I heered they was hirin men to run the trip to Newer'Leans [New Orleans] so I jumped the *C. B. Church* and went over to the *C. B. Kilbur.* That boat was named after John Kilbur, a rich shipping man from Kentucky. That was in the year '71 when I made my first trip to Newer'Leans. From then on I stayed on that run. We'd make the run in about every twenty to thirty days. As many years as I stayed on that run, I never had a fight in my life. Now you wanter know how I was able to do that, don't you? In the first place I stayed outer argyments [*sic*], cause I felt this way: at first I said to myself, 'I'm mongst Negroes who knows what it's all about cause they been free longer than I was. Here I come from one of the worse slave states, Virginia, and these men from up above the line.' Well, I couldn't do nuthin argyin with them. They knowed more'n I did. That bein the case I could learn more by lis'ning, which I did. Then when I did ketch on I found out that argyin didn't git ya no where cause you wasn't gonner 'suade the other feller no how an he wasn't gonner git you to see like him. There you are. It's jes like eatin soup with a fork. So from one year to another I never got in a fuss and I never had a fight.

"Now to come back to my buddie, Jimmie Harris. He was doin fine, yes, sir, he made a fine soldier but somehow I never did have the urge agin to go back to join the army—even after my two years was up. But I used to always hear from Jimmie. He would write from where ever he was and tell me how he was doin. Round about this time the war on the Indians had started and I got a letter from him sayin they had sent his comp'ny under General [George A.] Custer and that they was gonner fight Sittin Bull and his devilish Indians. Man, they was raisin sand then. They had broke off the Reservations and was killin up everything in sight. So the Government sent troops under General [George] Crook, General [John] Gibbon, General [Marcus] Reno and General Custer to set Sittin Bull in his place. The las letter I got from Jimmie said they was movin west to git out in the 'bad lands' and he wrote somthin that I'll remember til this day. There was in General Custer's army a Negro scout by the name of 'Niggers Mose Tom.' He was one of the bes' scouts that Custer had and after scoutin around up there in that Indian Country he come back and told Custer that he couldn't take Sittin Bull then cause he was too strong. He told him that the Sioux, that's Sittin Bull's tribe, had everything, includin rifles. They wasn't usin bows and arrows an spears any more, but they had been gittin guns from somewheres. Then he told Custer that there was too many Indians for him to handle alone. He said it must been nearly 15,700 Indians with Sittin Bull. But Custer didn't take his advice. No, from somewheres else a official report comes that Sittin Bull had divided up his Indians and he was in the neighborhood of the Little Big Horn River. Well, sir, that's the las I ever heard of Jimmie. He wrote and said, 'Well, we're off. Wish me luck.' I did, but it didn't do him any good. Cause nobody was left to tell the tale. Some say Custer thought he was creepin up on Sittin Bull's camp in the dark. An the men was comin through the woods when what they thought was logs was Indians wrapped up in blankets, 15,000 of em an not a soul was left to tell the tale. That's how I say that the army man saved my life when he turned me down 'cause I would have been with General Custer when he made his last stand. That muster been in '76 cause I went back to Cincinnati and that's where I heard the news. I was really hurt cause in all the years after I never had a friend like Jimmie. Most a the time I was a lone wolf. I traveled up and down that Mississippi River for well nigh fifty-six years. I was a fireman for twenty-four years and I was a hillman for thirty-two years. Well, you see, a hillman is an ace deck hand. He gotter know how to load and how to unload, and how to handle freight. Young man, I usedter [*sic*] be able to handle a bale of cotton jes like you'd handle a pillow slip. I was fireman on the *R. E. Lee*. Yes, the same *Robt. E Lee* what run the race with the *Natchez*. I remember all the people when we left Newer'Leans and they jes crowded the shore. Every place where we passed through there was people lined up to see us go by. Mr. Kilbur and those men had their money up too. No, Sir, we never did get behind. After we left I don't remember nuthin much 'cause the cap'n was callin for steam and more steam. An I was putting it there, too, 'cause I could go with the best of em. Yes, sir, we got out in front and stayed there til we hit St. Louis.

"Well, now, that's a question which has got jes four answers to it 'cause I jes about come nigh losin my life four times I well remember. The first time I was off the boat jes outer Vicksburg and I was waitin on the river bank for the foreman to come and git me so we could go to Vicksburg in a skiff. So while I was waitin I thought I'd take a nap under a tree. When all of a sudden I thought I had a creepy feeling and I woke up with a jump and looked right inter this big black panther's eyes. And when I jumped he sprang for me. Looker here, see those marks. They're all the way across from this arm across my chest to this arm. See where those big claws jes ripped me open. And til this day I don't know what saved my life. It was an act of providence, but that big black devil left me alone. The foreman found me and took me to the hospital.

"The next three times I nearly lost my life was on three boats. I had three of them to sink and I was on them. There was the *C. B. Church*, the *Valley Queen* and the *West O'Ville* and I couldn't swim a lick, but I managed to git in one of the boats.

"Long afterwards I started makin short runs up the Red River. Then I spent many years in the Marine Service and after I took sick I had to stay in the hospital for a long time. But when I got well they sent me here. Since I didn't have no kin people. Well, I did have a sister who was sixty-two years old when I went back to visit Charlottesville, but she was dribling and talkin outer her head. She was old an feeble at sixty-two. Well, I don't have much now but I have a trunk, two good suits. I don't have no jewelry like I used to. I used to have a gold watch chain three and a half feet long and I always had three or four hundred dollars in my pockets, but now I thank God I'm still alive and I know I'm gonner live a good while longer.

"The thing I'm most proud of? Well, it's not hard to tell but it's this: In my traveling sometimes I'd take a few weeks off and go to the east but I'd git homesick for the river and come back. But in my traveling up and down the river and in the east in Ohio and in Kentucky and in Illinois and Michigan I have come to see and know by sight thirteen presidents of the United States. I saw Grant right after he took Richmond. I saw Jeff Davis, McKinley, Fil[l]more, Pierce, J. Buchanan, Johnson, Garfield, Old Teddy Roosevelt, then there was Taft, Wilson and Harding. I saw all of them. But ya know the strangest thing of all [was that] I never did see Abe Lincoln. Somehow I never did run across him. I don't know why. That's something to be proud of ain't it? Yes sir thirteen Presidents of the United States and I've seen em all!"

ELLEN BROOMFIELD

Age: 88
1326 Franklin Street, New Orleans, Louisiana
February 20, 1941

Hobbling along with her full old-fashioned calico dress, almost touching the ground, her arms and hands, filled with her morning's gleanings, we greeted this old Mammy of a by-gone day with:

"Well, Auntie, it's refreshing to see one like you, with your long skirt and bonnet."

"Whut I want to wear short dresses for? I don' hav' to show 'em, besides the way some of these women's dresses is an insult to God who created them, an' that's why mens got so little respec' these days, an' it's all they own fault too.

"I was born way bac' yonder in 1853 in slavery time an' my Pa an' Ma had 19 chil'ren—all by the same Pa and Ma— an' we wus raised right, never went to any dances, but played 'Ring-round-rosy' an' things like that, an' I raised my chil'ren like that too."

We sat on the steps of her lodging where she deposited her sack of coal which she had picked up across the R.R.

tracks and her basket with several discarded tobacco boxes, which she could "fin' use for some pieces of kindlint [*sic*]" to "Start the fire with[,]" an old bottle and other miscellany which she had picked up in her morning's meanderings. "Aunt Ellen" is of the ante-bellum type and "we reckoned without our host" when we expected a good story from her.

"I jes' don' know anythin'—no signs, no songs, nothin'—

"Chillun in my day were never 'lowed round grown folks when they was talkin'. We played an' were happy. Seems like we didn't get sick much then. In Spring they giv' us sulphur an' molasses to purify our blood an' candy was made out [of] Jimson weed an' sugar an' that was good for worms.

"When folks had too much blood they cupped them. Well, it was like this:

"You take a cup of water an' put in it a piece of cotton, put to temple and set cotton on fire, that draws blood. Saw my Ma do it many a time.

"There were 19 chil'ren in our family an' we had to work as soon as we were big enough. I use to plow, it was hard, but it may be that's what made me so so [*sic*] strong. We had plenty sweet 'taters. Seems like they don't have good ones now. All were red an' when roasted they dripped out a kinder syrup. Now they call 'em yams, but you don't often see them. We didn't eat those ol' 'nigger chokers'. If they were planted they were given to the swine.

"Maybe it was because we were more careful in tendin' then. After the diggin' an' the earth got nat'ral like, it was plowed over and after a few weeks it was plowed again; after a while the plantin' was made, an' we kep' all weeds out an' the 'taters were good.

"Sunday mornin' we got up early an' washed our feets, an' scrubbed up so's to get to Sunday school which was a long way off, an' we went barefoot."

"Aunt Ellen," or as such she would have been called a few generations, has little history. Her life may be called a prosaic one, but she is happy. She says she is and her looks do not belie her words. Hers is the simple faith that could remove mountains. She sings:

> My Jesus is a rock in a weary lan'
> A weary lan', a weary lan'
> My Jesus is a rock in a weary [land]
> A shelter in the time of storm."

HENRIETTA BUTLER

Age: over 80
511 Wag[n]er Street, Gretna, Louisiana
Interviewer: Flossie McElwee

"Ise eighty some odd years ole, born at La Fouche [La-fourche Parish], my Ma's name Easter—dat her picture over dare. I was born in slavery. Ise not ashame' to tell it either, an' known somethin' about it.

"My dam ol' Missus was mean as hell. You see dis finger here?—dare is where she bit it de day us was set free. Never will forget how she said 'Come here, you little black bitch you!' and grabbed my finger—almos' bit it off. Her 'ole name was Emily Haidee. When she found out we was goin' to be free she raised all kind of hell; de Boss could do nothin' at all with her. She had two big saddle horses—one name Canaan, the other name Bill. She got on ole Bill and come to New Orleans few days befo' us was sat free, an' when de Boss fetched her back she was in a black box. He buried her in de field—he didn' have no respec' for her[;] she was too mean. I know ever' night I had to wash dat ole woman's foots an' rub dem fo I could ever go home to bed.

"I knows the day dem Sojer's came in, taken' all de

meat out of de smoke house, got all de chickens an' turkeys. She raised hell with the Boss an' tol' him to run dem son of bitches away. He didn' say air [any] thing to dem sojers 'cause he was too scared.

"She made me have a baby by one of dem mens on de plantation. De ole devil! I gets mad ever' time I think about it. Den dey took de man to war. De baby died, den I had to let dat ol devil's baby suck dese same tiddies hanging right here. She was allus knockin' me around. I worked in the house nursin'.

"We allus had plenty of vegetables, salt[,] meal, corn bread, hominy grits. Us didn' know whut biscuit was. All de slaves on de plantation got vegetables from de Bosse's [sic] garden. We never went to church, or no place—didn' know it was such a thing. You know none of the white folks didn't want the niggers to get out, they was afraid they would learn somethin'. They made my Ma have babies all de time; she was sellin' the boys and keepin' the gals.

"Her old brother was a doctor. He would give us pills when we got sick. I remember one day one of the mens had lock-jaw. That ol' woman made a fly blister, and put [it] on dat poor nigger and let it stay until it blistered. Then took a stiff brush and roughed over dat sore place an' when she did dat nigger hallowed [hollered] and his jaws come unlocked.

"After I was free I picked shrimp, worked in the Dago gardens, washed an' ironed for de white folk. Ise too ol' to do any thing now—been lookin' for the Governor to give me some money, but he aint yet."

MANDA COOPER

Age: over 100
Cut off Road, Algiers, Louisiana

"I was born in North Carlonia [*sic*] on Jessie Jinks plantation. I was in the field pulling the hoe when my young Master was sent to war. Mr. Jessie was my older Master [and] young Jessie was one of my Bosses too. I am over a hundred yrs old. Miss Shad was my Mistress[.] They were allus good to me. I never did get a whipping but I have seen some [of] the nigger beat until they would be bleeding. I never did have no children. I was sold from my maw [and] all my brothers and sister was sold. The man that bought me said he was going to bring us where the money grew on trees and you no [know] what that was? Picking Moss. That man kept me until peace declared. Martha, Ad'line, Annie, Carlina, and Tilda are all the sister I can remember. I just sit here and wonder sometimes what become of them. I have no kin no where here. We allus had plenty to eat during slavery time[. W]e sho' did work hard for what us got tho. I can remember my Mistress making me a dress and it was yellow[,] made the dye out of green pecans. I worked in the wheat fields, Tobacco, Rye[,] barley and oats, we raised all kinds of vegetables and fruit, we did not work so hard in the winter time for it was to[o] cold[. T]he old Mistress would have the cellar stored with grub for the Winter. I seen times when you would wake up [and] the snow would be up to the door. We did not have all that many clothes to wear so we had to stay in. [A]fter I come here and was sot free I got married just common law[,] not like they marry now. I had to work in the rice fields, cain [sic] plantation and done every thing a woman could do. But I never did have no children[. Y]ou can ask any of the white folks around here and they will tell you I have all ways been a good nigger. I never went to school[,] never did go to church until after peace declared. If the Mistress caught any of the Nigger thinking about calling on the Lord they were whipped. I live right here in this one room shack by myself. I have one God child. He is sixty yrs old[,] he comes around and cooks for me[,] he is all cripple up[,] he use to be a cook on a boat. He ain't give me no breakfast are [or] dinner yet[. H]e says it takes time to cook any thing right. The welfare is taking care of me. God only noes [knows] what I would do if it was not for that. Hard as I have worked during my life[,] was a slave and every thing[,] looks like I could be some where that I could be taken care of but the peoples don't want to bother with old folks. I carry a little Insurance to bury me with. I no [know] when I was young[,] people did not bury like they do now, all the slaves were buried on the plantation. I remember going to one funeral during slavery days. The boss[,] he got up and said a few words[,] they throwed the dirt in and all of us went back to the fields hoeing. My

Maw never worked in the fields[. S]he had a baby every year [and] she had twens [twins] one time, so the old Master taken care of her[. S]he bought [*sic*] him more money having children than she could working in the field. None of us had the same father[. T]hey would pick out the bigest [*sic*] Nigger and tell her they wanted a kid by him. She had to stay with him until she did get one. When I got old enough to Breed and never could have no children I stayed in the field. The old Mistress would all ways have two are [or] three barrels of apple cider in the cellar made out of the peeling and cores. When the young boss come from war they would have a big party for him but us Nigger Never did no [know] what they done[. W]e never did have no meat to eat[,] only once a month[. T]hey said meat was not good for you. The first money I ever made I bought me a piece of Salt Meat and eat that with turnip greens and corn Bread. I have asthma now [and] have to smoke fig leaves. I am so poor until my bones are pushing threw [*sic*] the skin. I gess they will push on threw befo I die."

MARTIN DRAGNEY

Age: 79
1408 Dumaine Street, New Orleans, Louisiana
Interviewer: Posey
February 25, 1939

"I was born May 11th 1860, at 11 o'clock in the morning. That's what my Grandma told me and I never forgot it—for she told it so often and she lived to be 114 years old— and she was a midwife.

"My Pa's Pa was named Martin Dragney and he was never a slave. They used to call him a free-man-of-color, and he had lots of money.

"He was born in Little Chiapas in Mexico where his people were living. And he went around the country building gin-houses and upright mills for turning out rollers to grind sugar-cane and he made lots of money, for they needed those things in that day. He learned all these things in Mexico where he was born and raised.

"And one time when he was in New York a vessel landed somewhere on the Hudson River. And the Holland Dutch had brought over a lot of negroes from Cape Town, Africa, which they had stolen. They seized them when they were totin [carrying] water from the river and these Dutch people put them on a sailing vessel.

"In that time it took about six months to sail to this country, for they had to go round the Isthmus.

"And, these Dutch people sold their cargo to the Indians for 100 pounds of Tobacco each one—and my Grandpa bought my Grandma for $100.00 and she was only fourteen years old—and he brought her to New Orleans—and he told me that was the year after the Stars fell [the famous Leonid meteor shower took place in 1833–34]—and he said that people were running around crying and begging people to pray for them. White and colored, all alike—They thought it was Judgment Day."

Three Wives

"And my Grandpa put my Grandma with his other two wives in his house which he owned at No. 40 Roman St., the other side [of] Girod Graveyard near the Basin.

"And during the War my Pa and my Ma were separated and I remained with my Grandpa."

Betrayed By Son

"And when the War came on the Yankees use to give us hard-tack and we run to get it. We thought they was giving us cake.

"And one time my Pa was hiding up a chimney and they

called me and asked me where he was. I was only a little fellow and I didn't know any better so I told them. And they captured him and put him in battle at Mansfield, La."

A Sailor He Was

"And after I grew up I was in the sailor-life. I went on an iron-clad Brigatine [*sic*] where I stayed for 1 year and 18 months. It was a trading-vessel to East India, Bombay and Calcutta. It was hauling tea, hides and pearl rocks like they make teeth, buttons and such things out of.

"Nineteen of us enlisted here in New Orleans and when [our] time was up they didn't bring us back like they said, but left us in Philadelphia and we got the Chief of Police and the Mayor to see if they couldn't make them pay our way back home. They did too. And we came in over the Chatanooga [*sic*] R.R. and we sure was glad to get back.

"As a roustabout and common laborer—I used to make $1.50 a day.

"I married a silly young girl—and we had one child. And then she left me, said I was too old for her. And I was 31 years old—I never married again but I had three more children.

"I ain't a member of any church but I like the Baptist best of all and maybe I'll get converted and join it. I don't know.

"I never went to school so I have no education. But I used to count stock and keep a record, and I can count money without any mistake.

"I never could sing so I don't know any songs. I was never a hand to go around much.

"I used to go out fishing in Lake Pontchartrain, opposite Spanish Fort, and I would see those voudoo [*sic*] people dance for the white people—They paid them money to dance—the konk konk dance. They were only half dressed. They wore the britch-cloth [breechcloth] and hollered and jumped about like they was crazy—and they had tambourines and drums and jawbones of jackasses.

"Now I'm on Relief and I pay rent for my room and live out [off] the rest."

MRS. M. S. FAYMAN

Age: 87
Cherry Heights near Baltimore, Maryland
Interviewer: Rogers
November 3, 1937

[Note: In colonial French and Spanish Louisiana, free people of color were one-sixth the population. Social status was more important than race. French was the primary language, and French-speaking slaves were in demand. Le Code Noir limited free people of color from voting or holding public office, but they were free to prosper as landowners, slave owners, merchants, and craftsmen. Their social and religious lives were similar to those of all other free citizens. As tension heightened on the eve of the Civil War and most states outlawed the entry of free people of color, the Louisiana legislature eliminated many of their liberties. They could no longer assemble or form organizations. They could not testify against whites and were required to carry passes and observe curfews. They were at risk of being captured as slaves, as happened to Mrs. Fayman at age ten.]

"I was born in St. Nazaire Parish [a church parish] in

Louisiana, about 60 miles south of Baton Rouge, in 1850. My father and mother were Creoles, both of them were people of wealth and prestige in their day and considered very influential. My father's name was Henri de Sales and mother's maiden name [was] Marguerite Sanchez De Haryne. I had two brothers[,] Henri and Jackson[,] named after General Jackson, both of whom died quite young, leaving me the only living child. Both mother and father were born and reared in Louisiana. We lived in a large old spacious house surrounded by flowers and situated on a farm containing about 750 acres, on which we raised pelicans for sale in the market at New Orleans.

"When I was about 5 years old I was sent to a private school in Baton Rouge, conducted by French sisters, where I stayed until I was kidnapped in 1860. At that time I did not know how to speak English; French was the language spoken in my household and by the people in the parish.

"Baton Rouge, situated on the Mississippi, was a river port and stopping place for all large river boats, especially between New Orleans and large towns and cities [to the] north. We children were taken out by the sisters after school and on Saturdays and holidays to walk. One of the places we went was the wharf. One day in June and on Saturday a large boat was at the wharf going north on the Mississippi River. We children were there. Somehow, I was separated from the other children. I was taken up bodily by a white man, carried on a boat, put in a cabin and kept there until we got to Louisville, Kentucky, where I was taken off.

"After I arrived in Boulaville [?] I was taken to a farm near Frankfort and installed there virtually a slave until

1864, when I escaped through the kindness of a delightful Episcopalian woman from Cincinnati, Ohio. As I could not speak English, my chores were to act as a tutor and companion for the children of Pierce Buckran Haynes, a well known slave trader and plantation owner in Kentucky. Haynes wanted his children to speak French and it was my duty to teach them. I was the private companion of 3 girls and one small boy, each day I had to talk French and write French for them. They became very proficient in French and I in the rudiments of the English language.

"I slept in the children's quarters with the Haynes' children, ate and played with them. I had all the privileges of the household accorded me with the exception of one, I never was taken off nor permitted to leave the plantation. While on the plantation I wore good clothes, similar to those of the white children. Haynes was a merciless brutal tyrant with his slaves, punishing them severely and cruelly both by the lash and in the jail on the plantation.

"The name of the plantation where I was held as a slave was called Beatrice Manor, after the wife of Haynes. It contained 8000 acres, of which more than 6000 acres were under cultivation, and having about 350 colored slaves and 5 or 6 overseers[,] all of whom were white. The overseers were the overlords of the manor; as Haynes dealt extensively in tobacco and trading in slaves, he was away from the plantation nearly all the time. There was located on the top of the large tobacco warehouse a large bell, which was rung at sun up, twelve o'clock and at sundown, the year round. On the farm the slaves were assigned a task to do each day and in the event it was not finished they were severely whipped.

While I never saw a slave whipped, I did see them after-wards, they were very badly marked and striped by the over-seers who did the whipping.

"I have been back to the farm on several occasions, the first time in 1872 when I took my father there to show him the farm. At that time it was owned by Colonel Hawkins, a Confederate Army officer.

"Let me describe the huts, these buildings were built of stone, each one about 20 feet wide, 50 feet long, 9 feet high in the rear, about 12 feet high in front, with a slanting roof of chestnut boards and with a sliding door, two windows be-tween each door[,] back and front[,] about 2 x 4 feet, at each end a door and window similar to those on the side. There were ten such buildings, to each building there was another building 12 x 15 feet. This was where the cooking was done. At each end of each building there was a fire place built and used for heating purposes. In front of each building there were barrels filled with water supplied by pipes from a large spring, situated about 300 yards on the side of a hill which was very rocky, where the stones were quarried to build the buildings on the farm. On the outside near each window and door there were iron rings firmly attached to the walls, through which an iron rod was inserted and locked [at] each end every night, making it impossible for those inside to escape.

"There was one building used as a jail, built of stone about 20 x 40 feet with a hip roof about 25 feet high, 2-story. On the ground in each end was a fire place; in one end a small room, which was used as office; adjoining, there was another room where the whipping was done. To reach the second story there was built on the outside, steps leading to a door, through which the female prisoners were taken to the room. All of the buildings had dirt floors.

"I do not know much about the Negroes on the plantation who were there at that time. Slaves were brought and taken away always chained together, men walking and women in ox carts. I had heard of several escapes and many were captured. One of the overseers had a pack of 6 or 8 trained blood hounds which were used to trace escaping slaves.

"Before I close let me give you a sketch of my family tree. My grandmother was a Haitian Negress, grandfather a Frenchman. My father was a Creole. After returning home in 1864, I completed my high school education in New Orleans in 1870, graduated from Fisk University [in] 1874, taught French there until 1883, married Prof. Fayman, teacher of history and English. Since then I have lived in Washington, New York, and Louisiana. For further information, write me c/o Y.W.C.A. (col.), Baltimore, to be forwarded."

REBECCA FLETCHER

Age: 98, born 1837
Iberville Street, New Orleans, Louisiana
Interviewer: Posey
August 21, 1940

Ninety-eight years, we tell Rebecca[,] is a good age, more than the Biblical one. "Yes'm hit is," she replies. "I've been through a whole lot an' I'm still livin'. You don' fin' many people bo'n befo' freedom.

"I wuz jus' this mornin' tellin' my son's wife how we made gravy without flour durin' the War, it's good for these young folks to know what we went through."

"Well, we would like to know too, won't you tell us?"

"Jus' take yo' meant [*sic*] an' fry it, po' water in it, cook grits to eat with water gravy an' co'n bread. The reason they didn't thicken it with flour is bekase there wasn't any, an' we had no bakin' powder either, so we took co'n cobs an' burn 'em, an' put the ashes in a jar an' put water on top an' put that in co'n bread, stid [instead] of bakin'-powder.

"Slaves had to go to fiel' befo' daybre'k and didn't come

home till after dark. Then they cooked dinner and lunch to take with 'em nex' day.

"The chil'ren were lef behin', an' ole woman had the care of 'em and it was in a big kitchen, where she cooked and fed 'em. That was in slavery times. After freedom, when the mothers worked for theyselves, they took the babies along to the fiel's and put a piece of fat meat in a cloth and tied it roun' like a tit. They put string to it an' fas'ened it to the big toe, so's if they tried to swaller it, their toe would jerk it out.

"When the war came on they conscripted men to go fight, white men. Some didn't want to go and they had they wives to hide 'em under a bed or in a chim'ley or some place to keep from gwine to war.

"They didn't have any automobiles then, they had a slave to drive 'em in a kerrige. Long 'bout that time, I heard people say dey wuz goin' to have kerriges go without horses. I couldn't on'erstand that, so I thought they meant that mules would take their places. But hit's come to pass—an' when I saw the fus' one I got on my knees an' said, 'Lor', Lor', Thy ways are pas' findin' out.'"

We told her that hundreds of years before even she was born, there was an old woman who made prophesies—and was known as "Mother Shipton." Strange to say nearly every prediction had come to pass including this.

> Carriages without horses will go,
> In eighteen hundred and ninety-four.

"Yes'm, that's whut I heered talk of[,] kerriges would go without hosses.

"Like what I wuz sayin'. The ole slave woman in the kitchen used to sing hymns, you call 'em spirituals, now—but ennyhow, she would sing and soon even the littlest one learned from her and joined in. One of these was:

> Dark was the night an' col' the groun'
> On which our Lord was laid.
> Great drops of sweat like blood poured down,
> An' anchored kneeled [*sic*] he prayed!

"An' she sang another like this:

> Min' my sister how you step on the cross,
> Yo foot might slip an' yo' soul ud be los'.

"In slavery days, we were not allowed to visit other plantations. The onliest way was to go to ol' marster an' gitten him to write a paper with his name signed to hit sayin' we could pass. Those paddy-rollers wuz mighty bad about pickin' you up. They used to be a song: 'Run nigger run, the paddy rollers ketch you.'

"When the las' gun wuz shot, a man came through the quarters where we were an' when we saw him we wonnered who he wuz. He wuz dressed in [a] blue suit trimmed with brass buttons. He come up to a woman sittin' on the grass eatin' her dinner, an' he axed her for some of hit an' she tol' him:

" 'I ain' got no dinner for you, you ol' loafer, marster giv' me this dinner an' I'm hungry. Go 'long.'

"He didn't want her dinner, he wuz jes' talking. So then

he went to where the big crows wuz an' said: 'You all are free. Pick up the hoe an' the plows, take 'em to [the] right places. Feed the mules an' go away like I say, 'cause you's free an' can do as you please, now an' forever, and forever.'

"Some went right away, or as soon as they git their things together, others didn't want to leave an' staid straight on. But marster tol' us to go. He said he couldn't take keer of us, that times had changed an' he had no money lef'.

"I never wuz whipped in my life by anyone. I wuz always good an' did like they tol' me.

"Some of those overseers were mean men. They wanted slaves to have babies bekase they wuz valuable, so when a slave wuz erbout to produce a baby, an' he wanted her whupped, he had a hole dug in the groun an' made her lay acrost it an' her han's and foots were tied, so she had to submit quiet like to the beatin' with a strop.

"I hear tell that when a 'omon [woman] was a bornin' a chile, that death wen' roun' her bed seven times, a studyin' whether he'd take her or not. I got three chillun livin' an' I don' know how many dead, so I reckun he had pleny chances at me.

"After freedom, when we were on our own account we had a hard time. We made our own soap by savin' bones an' greasy stuff to make soap. We put oak an' hickry ashes in a bar'l [sic] an' made holes in it an' poured rain water on top an' let hit drop through ashes. This made lye. We cooked the fats in this lye slowly, an' it wuz so strong it would eat yo' han' ef you used much of it. After cooking enough we put this mixture in molds and when it wuz col' we cut it in cakes.

"We made lye hominy erbout the same way. We took

corn, not the kind you eat, but lak you feed hosses an' cook it in lye made out of hic'ry or oak ashes an' when the hulls peel off an' you can wash it in col' water hit's ready to eat, an' hits good, too."

Blue-Mass Pills

"Ole Missis useter give us blue mass pills [a drug "made by rubbing up metallic mercury with confection of roses until all the globules disappear"] when we needed medicine. It sho did make us sick. We had to get sick to get well, ole Missis said.

"Dat 'possum[,] it am good to eat, karve it to de heart. Hit's difrent—a coon an' a 'possum—bekase a coon has musk in it an' ef yo' don' tak' hit out hit's bitter an' not fitten to eat. The musk is in a lil' sack un'er front fore-feet an' hin' leg.

" 'Possum ain' thet way, so you wet a cloth an' wrap 'possum in hot ashes so's to tak' skin off, an' when skin comes off the meat will be jes' as white an' nice lookin'. Then you wash him in strong salt water, so's to take away wil' [wild] taste. After a day or night (ef yo' ken wait thet long) yo' kin parboil him, then bake him. Have 'taters roasted along to eat.

"When I wuz lil' l heard 'em sing:

> Sit down chile, sit down,
> Sit down chile, sit down,
> Sit down chile, sit down,
> O, Lord, I can't sit down!

> O, Lord, I fol' up my arms an' I wonder,
> An' I wonder Lord, I wonder,
> I fol' up my arms an' wonder to see,
> How far I am away from my home.

"Another wuz lak this:

> I saw the light comin' down,
> I saw the light comin' down,
> Hit's a mighty pretty light comin' down,
> Way up in the heavens comin' down.

"They don' have singin' thet way enymo'. There's another verse erbout 'I can't sit down, I want my starry crown.'

"Friday is the day the jay-bird carries a grain of san' to the bad man to torment you, if you died bad. If you lived without thinkin' about God, those sands will help to worry you, for they are hot and will burn your feet.

"If you ask for a cool drink of water, they give you brimstone an' hot lead. Old bad man's a person who wuz quarrelsome in heaven an' God threw him out because he wanted to be another God. He wuz jealous. He couldn't be punished eternally so he was made a king over the bad place. I know what he looks like 'cause I've seen pictures of him, an' he shows two horns, an' a tail, an' a suit in red, an' he has big eyes an' uses a pitchfork to keep folks from gettin' across the river."

"Rebecca tell me just what you expect to see when you enter the pearly gates?"

"That's right, the pearly gates. I expect to see my Saviour with my long white robe ready to throw hit aroun' me an' a crown in His han' to put on my head, it'll be full of stars, too. Slippers? Yes'm golden slippers, an' I'll walk the golden streets too. No'm, the slippers won' hurt my feet at all, bekase the Bible says there'll be no pain or suf'rin' in heaven." With that she looked down at her worn pieces of leather held together with strings and which flapped at every step. No more pain or suffering. No, not even the tired, aching feet that had walked the stony paths when even Sunday shoes were unknown. "No mo' pain or sufrin'—for all God's chilluns got shoes." We reminded her. "Yes'm mebbe so, but He said slippers."

Rebecca is 98 and "disremembers," but when you tell her that you will be back and that you want her to think over old times, she generally has something new to unfold, and so while her story must come in fragments—it is as she tells it. . . .

"I remember when the soljers passed on the big road in Centreville, Miss. They marched with guns over their shoulders, a blanket an' a canteen, with water in hit. You could hear 'em comin' miles away. It sounded lak a storm. They were Confidrate soljers an' there wuz two riders, one behin', an' one in front. It took 'em a whole day to pass, they wuz so many. No ma'm, we wan't scared of them, for they look kind!"

Rebecca lives with a daughter-in-law, and her wants are provided for by her son who sends her money, she says. She does all her own washing and is immaculately clean.

Her chief sorrow is in being away from her church—her church way back in the country where her membership is. She attends one near her, but it's entirely too fashionable. The preacher too, doesn't preach like old times and the congregation don't have a chance to sing. The choir does that "and it's high-filutin'."

They have a fine organ, a "pipe-organ they calls hit an' they wear night gowns."

But as she says she wants "watch-care"—so she [af]filiates with this church, but she wants her own pastor to preach her funeral sermon which he has promised to do.

She tells you of present day conditions which she thinks are shocking—in that preachers charge for "buryin' you."

"They surely do, whatever they think you can pay—five or ten dollars. An' they didn't uster do that. An' in ole times people called theyse'ves Christians, now they say they are church members."

ANNIE FLOWERS

Age: unknown
Theaid Street, McDonoghville, Louisiana
Interviewer: Flossie McElwee

"I'se been living here for about twelve yrs. Don't know jest how old I'es, but shore is been here a long time tho'.

"All I'se ever knowed was to work. Was borned on Mr. Gain's plantation.

"Was raised in the sugarcane fields. Was jest a small child when my mother was set free. Don't remember much about it. The day my maw was set free another Negro shoved her in the Futch canal. Dat's about all I can think off [*sic*].

"I'se got two chellum. My son Lu went to war, and died after coming home.

"This two chaps that is with me now is my great-grand children. Their ma got burned up over [in] town.

"Worked in the sugarcane fields all my life, bare-feeted and half naked. I didn't work for a salary, it was something to eat and a few rags to wear. We allus had Sunday off to play tho'. I married a good man and when he works, he always fetch the money home to me. He ain't worked in a long time. He got cut off of the W.P.A. Ain't never went back on yet.

"I takes in a few washing, but times shore is tough with us and these little children. You see, we have not got much of a shack to live in and so jambed up.

"I believes in the Lawd tho', I'se a member of the Saint Paul Babt Church but ain't been there in three long years—no clothes and shoes to wear.

"The white people sho' good to me tho', they give me old clothes for theses chillum. You see, I'se done got too old to work much, but that man I married sho' has been good and he worked hard too. My maw died soon after I married, I thank the Lawd, that I was not left a orphan like theses [*sic*] chillum.

"We jest sats down some times and talks about how we use to cut dat cane in them fields, in de heat and cold. I knows it was happier times than now, hearing all them Negro singing them old corn songs.

"They kindly went like this:

> Rains comes wit [wet] me.
> Sun comes dry me.
> Stand back boss man,
> Don't come nigh me.

"I'es forgot jest how it did go, we use to sang dat song about, 'Plow Gang, Plow in the Low Land!'

"But so much trouble has done went over dis head, I jest can't think.

"My son was allus good to me. When he died, the Government gived me his bonus—that was spent long time ago.

"Never went to school a day in my life, never had time. Work was all I knew to do. And I'es still trying to work."

CECEIL GEORGE

Age: 94
1521 Columbus Street, New Orleans, Louisiana
Interviewer: Maude Wallace
February 15, 1940

Life in Slavery Days

Sister George, who lives with her daughter Rebecca Coleman, is quite aged. As near as they can figure out she has already "made ninety-four."

She was seated on a low stool when I entered her room—a room that is plainly furnished, with an iron bed, a homemade dresser, a table, two straight chairs and a large rocking chair that sits by the one small window, where she evidently spends most of her time.

She is very dark and wrinkled, her eyes are blurred and her hands are old. She is quite stout, uses a cane, and due to trouble with her feet and old age, needed my assistance to "get to her rocking chair," which was only three or four steps.

She was dressed in cotton, an old jacket, and a dark kerchief on her head.

When she speaks, there is not a trace of bitterness in her voice and always reverence for "De Lawd."

"I'se lived in dis country mos' a my life, but I was borned an' raised in de ole country at the Great Swamp Plantation, in Charleston County, South Carolina.

"It was a beautiful place—great big. In de ole country (South Carolina) we raised cotton most, an' rice an' corn.

"Our folks in de Big House were fine people, all born with de gold spoon in dere mouth. Dere we had a church right on de plantation,—go dere all de time, but twice a month, dey'd take us to town to de Big Church,—all de blacks an' de whites together.

"We'd sing an' go at our work in de fields real happy. We had our own little gardens, an' we had all we wanted, but de Master he died, an' de young son, he wanted his share o' de plantation, so dey had to sell half o' everything.

"De Missus an' her daughter, dey kept de big house an' some o' de slaves, but some o' us had to go,—dey sold us like a gang o' chickens—My whole family, an' plenty more. I remember well, we all cried to leave de ole country, but we had more tears dan dat to shed.

"Well dey paid de young Massa his half o' de money, dat is part o' it—an' was to pay de rest, every year, so much every year,—but freedom come, an' he was shut out.

"Dey sold us to Dick Proctor, his plantation down here named de Florizone, in St. Bernard Parish.

"We come here on de ship, dis was before de War an' I remembers it well. I was about twelve years ole den. I can see us now, riding on de water. One morning, we come out lookin' an' see nothin', but sky an' water, an' we had been used to pine trees everywhere, an', yo' listen, when we look, a person was sittin' in de water, on a rock, combing her hair an' singin'.—I called my father quick, I was afraid she'd get drowned,—but yo' know, who she is? A Maremaid (Mermaid) what lives in de water, half fish an' half woman. I get so scart (scared)—dey drag us in quick.

"Yes, I remember de water, dey made us go by de sea, because den we can't go back, God help us!

"We come to de mos' wicked country dat our God's son ever died for! De ole people used to cry—dear Lawd, how dey grieved! Dey never thought dey'd have to live in a heathern [*sic*] country—dey all dead now.

"Florizone was a big plantation, dey raise most sugar cane, dere was a big sugar house on de plantation, an' a great big house for de white people. It's good to have a fine house to live in, but if dey don' have de Christ, where de soul goin' to go? Dis is de dressing room, dere's no repentance in de grave.

"It was a big place, twenty houses in de quarters; all de houses packed wid people. Oh Lawd, I come up in hard times,—slavery times.

"Everybody worked,—young an' ole, if yo' could only carry two or three sugar cane yo' worked. No school, no church—yo' couldn't sing, an' Saturday night dey always have a dance, but yo' worked. Sunday, Monday, it all de same, an' if yo' say 'Lawd a' mercy'—de Overseer whip yo'. De ole people, dey jes' set down an' cry—it like a heathern part o' de country.

"Yo has to put yo' candle out early an' shut yo'self up. Den get up while it's still dark an' start to work.

"In de ole country (South Carolina), yo' never have a scratch. Dey never whips dere slaves. Lock dem up—yes— but don' whip dem. Down here, dey strip yo' down naked, an' two men hold yo' down an' whip yo' till de blood come— Crouel (cruel) Oh, Lawd.

"So mind I tell yo' what I seed wid my own eyes. De people take sick an' dey die, dey ain't no coffin for dem, dey take planks an' nail dem together like a chicken coop—yo' can see through it, an' it's too short, de neck's too long. So a man stand up on him an' jump on him—here—he broke his neck, an' it fall on his chest like dis. Den dey nail de top on an' one nail go in de brain. I see dat wid my own eyes. Den dey put dem in de wagon what dey haul de manure in[,] nobody wid dem—de people have to go to work—wicked part o' de country—wicked! wicked! wicked!

"A woman named Thomas, her father die, but she couldn't stay with him, dey make her go to de field an' dey tole a man to go dig a hole. She cried, but it don' do no good. Pore Christian got a hard road, but dey got de sparit [*sic*] o' Jesus on dere side.

"In de ole country (S.C.), dey had spinning wheels made dere own cloth—made gloves, caps for de head, sho' me. In dis country, dey give yo' de ole clothes, one pair shoes a year, no stockin's an' in de winter, sometimes yo' so cold—Lawd (Lord) have mercy! But dey make every chile on de plantation, tote sugar cane jes de same.

"When a woman has a baby, if she can't go to de field,

when de baby is nine days ole, she has to sit an' sew. My mother died blind, jes from dat.

"I tell yo' something, we were children, an' we didn't know[,] we was playing, an' we seen a man coming up de road. He was walkin' an' he had a wide, wide hat on, an' a carpet sack on his shoulder. In de field de people was workin' an my Uncle was de driver. We was in de road playin', an' de man got to like de corner, we say 'Who dat comin?' When he got close, we break an' run to the quarters. He say, 'Don' run, come back, I am yo' friend. How yo' all do?' But we ready to run, an' he reached in his sack, break up some hard tack, dey call it[,] an' give us all a piece, when he done, he wrote on a piece a paper an' give it to my Uncle, de driver. Den he say to us, 'Can yo' keep a secret, an' don' repeat?' We say 'Yes, sah.' He say, 'I come from yo' friend Abraham Lincoln, he say, "Hold yo' peace."' He took de map of de parish, an' I don' know when he walked back, maybe at night, but we don' see him no more.

"Den my Father, run off de plantation to de Barracks to go to de war. He was killed three months before we knew it, an' was buried in Chalmette. After that a Uncle, brought us up an' we had to stay in that heathen place till freedom come.

"I married down there, an' we lived in a place called Berried Village. My husban' made his own crop, an' all my children were born in de country. I had fourteen children, an' never made a miss wid one. Nine is dead, five girls is livin! I worked hard, an' sent my children to school. I never got no school. We all Baptist. I was Baptized in de ole country (S.C.).

"When we was in Berried Village, dere was a ole Democrat didn't like a bone in colored people, he wouldn't look at us. When he spoke to us [he] said 'a Nigger, dog, an' Alligator all looked alike.' His name was William Green an' his wife was named Jerry. De yaller fever came along, an' he sweat. He used to keep his money in a iron chest, an' ease out jes' enough money to run de house on to Mrs. Jerry, dat was his wife an' a good woman, den she get sick.

"De yaller fever was ragin'; every day coffins goin' to de graveyard, so he sent fo' a special doctor fo' Mrs. Jerry—his name was Dr. Levere, an' he had a crippled foot. Well de doctor, he took sick. Mrs. Jerry, she call me to her bed, she say: 'Oh Ceceil, I'm sick, I'm scart (scared) de doctor sick an' de medicine don' do no good. My husban' must not know, but can't yo' make me some tea? Do something.' But I was scart a Mr. Green, so I jes' prayed over her an' something said, 'Trust God, make dat tea.' I went out[,] got de grass, got some Indian Root, put it on to boil an' I got some whiskey. I say 'Fo' God's sake, I don' wanna be killed.' But I give her de tea, an' she don' sweat, so I cover her up an' I go git de guts out of a pumkin [*sic*], an' boil it with whiskey an' give it to her, an' she sweat de fever out. . . . Wid God's help I got her on her feet.

"Dr. Levere, he went crazy. Mr. Green tried to get some other doctor to come to him, but de doctor he laughed, said he was dying, an' wid all his chest a money, he couldn't help dat, he was goin' to Hell. No money could help him, dey couldn't pay his way out a Hell! Dat man died an' his Sparit hant (haunt) dat house. He come back like bulldogs, in de day time.

"When my husban' died, we came here to live, that's thirty-eight years ago. My five children all live here in de city, but I'd fly back to de ole country if I could,—but all de ole folks is gone. I know.

"Here [*sic*] dat radio music? I like dem songs,—church songs—but yo' know dere's more untrue in dat, that what dey used to sing[,] 'Take Jesus, for yur Council.' We need it right now, but some throw it away.

"Wait, I'll sing yo' a song from de ole country (S.C.) but I have to study—I'm gettin' ole. Wait.

Inching Along

I'm inchin' along, inchin' along,
Jesus is comin, bye an' bye!
Like de pore lowly worm,
I'm inchin' along,
Jesus is comin' bye an' bye!

When I was a sinner, jes' like yo',
Jesus is comin', bye an' bye!
I did not know, what I could do 'cause
Jesus is comin' bye an' bye.

With worry I was like some one dead,
Jesus is comin' bye an' bye!
An ache in my heart, an ache in my head.
Jesus is comin' bye an' bye! . . ."

MARY HARRIS

Age: 86
4609 Camp Street, New Orleans, Louisiana
Interviewer: Posey
October 28, 1940

Mary doesn't know her age, she will tell you to find it by adding that she was 11 years old when surrender came.

Her hair, which is "wrapped with cotton string" as was the custom in old days[,] is white and she is without a wrinkle (why can't they put on the market their recipe?).

She was patching an old dress, or what remained of it. As she scrutinized her handiwork, she remarked: "My old ma used to say:

" 'A patch by patch is friendly, but a patch on patch is 'bomination.'" But now that she's old and has no one able to help her she must resort to this " 'bomination," and she's proud to wear garments patched in the "friendly style."

She has no revenue, she tells you. She can't get "relief" because she has a son who is supposed to take care of her.

"He does the bes' he kin, but they won't give him any work. I don' know how he manages to pay the rent."

She runs the house for him and when there is cooking to be done she is there to do it.

"In the first place I was raised to not run around, and when I was ol' enough to do as I please I never had the desire."

The house of two rooms and a kitchen is immaculately clean. On the beds are quilts which she has made of no particular design[,] the scraps just "fittin in."

"Sure I remember slavery times. I was a big girl, turned eleven. I used to pull the fan that kep' off the flies while the white folks was eatin'. It wasn't hard work but my arms used to get tired—'specially at dinner when they set so long at the table. I made the fires and brought in kindlin-wood and carried out the hashes [*sic*].

"I never got a whippin' either, because I was good an' did my work an' never talked back. My ma tol' me she was brutally beaten an' she was bitter all her life."

We admitted that slavery was a most unfortunate thing—but that all masters were not cruel. Old slaves still tell of their love for "ole Miss" and "old Marse," and the loyalty and love existing between them could never have been created in rancous [rancorous] hearts.

"The plantation was owned by Mr. Gaudet [Adam Gaudet of Sugar Plantation in St. James Parish]—and I've hearn tell that Frenchmen were the hardest people an' almos' squee'd blood outen their slaves. With Americans, it was different so jes' set it down when you hear of brutal treatment that it was foreigners."

The day was growing to a close. We told her that we would come again and listen to her memories.

But we had reckoned without our host for when we returned as if standing guard, was the son.

"You wish to see my mother? I'm sorry but I cannot permit her to be interviewed.

"Slavery! Why are you concerned about such stuff? It's bad enough for it to have existed and when we can't forget it there is no need of rehashing it."

We explained that his mother's pastor had given us her name because of her marvelous memory of other days. That we were only trying to preserve, from the reminiscences of old people, white and colored[,] what they remembered or had heard from their parents, old songs [of] work and spirituals, customs, fables and things on that order. If they cared to talk about slavery, which most of them did, we were interested in hearing about it, but if they chose to steer clear of it that was all right.

"Bitter? Yes, I'm bitter—I have a right to be. My mother tells me about the brutality of those days, how they whipped unmercifully their slaves."

"But every slave-holder was not like that," we ventured.

"Yes'm, I'm bitter and the more I think about it the madder I get. Look at me[;] they say I could pass for white. My mother is bright too. And why? Because the man who owned and sold my mother was her father. But that's not all. That man I hate with every fibre of my body[,] and why? A brute like that who could sell his own child into unprincipled hands is a beast—The power, just because he had the power, and thirst for money."

He calmed down. "Lady[,] you mean all right and if you want you can see my mother." But after such a tirade we were afraid[,] deciding that "discretion was the better part of valor." It was our first experience with a madman!

ELIZABETH ROSS HITE

Age: 80-plus
Interviewer: McKinney

Mrs. Elizabeth Ross Hite is an inmate of the Louisiana Freedmen Asylum, 3100 Audubon St. [New Orleans] [She] thinks she is over eighty years old and contends that the government ought to take care of her. Mrs. Hites mother, Artemise Ros[s] was receiving a pension for the war services of her husband, Brooks Ross, but it was discontinued after her death. Mrs. Hite said that three government representatives had been to see her but to no avail. She was more anxious to talk about this than anything else, citing examples of why she should get some kind of a pension throughout the interview.

Mrs. Elizabeth Ross Hite is a square faced, dark complexioned person, weighing about one hundred pounds; stands approximately five feet four inches. She was gaudily attired in a pink gingham dress, black shoes with a white piece of cloth tied around her head. Her hair is gray and is falling out by the handful. Mrs. Hite is a very nervous type but was quite cooperative on this visit which was the third.

She attributed her nervous condition to worry and contends that it prevents her from recalling every thing that she knows happened during slavery. She was made very comfortable sitting in one of the reception rooms' rocking chairs.

"I was born on de Trinity Plantation dat Godchaux has bought since de war. Pierre Landro was de master. He came from France and was very rich. Mah mudder and father came from Richmond, Virginia. Dere name is Artemise and Brooks Ross. I had two brudders and one sister but dey is all dead now. Mah brudders' name was David Ross and Brook Ross. David was de oldest. Mah sister's name was Annette Ross. Mah mudder died in N'Awlins [New Orleans] wid de small pox. She took sick comin' after de gov'ment's money. Mah father was burried [*sic*] in de Fort Hutson graveyard in Baton Rouge whar he died. He asked de captain to put a tree on his grave so his children could find it but we nebber did bother.

"All mah kin people was house servants during slavery. Mah grandmudder, Mariah Lewis died since peace declared. I remember how mah grandmudder used to tell bout de hard times dey had but not us. We had a gud master. Dere was over one hundred head of hands on de place. Mah master was gud to all of dem. He nebber did whip dem but his overseers would. He was too rich and too busy making money and had no time to fool wid us darkies. He even told us so. Yas sir, he sold ev'rything dat was produced on de plantation. Mah master christianed [*sic*] all of his children in de Catholic church and bought clothes by de carloads. He had thirty-five plantations but sold ev'ryone of dem when he heard dat de Yankees was comin'. One day I heahed mah master say, 'You darkies is gwine to hav a hell of a time getting along wid dem Yankees. Dey is de meanest people on earth. Dey won't be as kind to ya as I is. I um not gwine to let dem kill me so I um gwine to get away from heah.' He saved his money and put it in big boxes.

"We slept on wooden beds wid fresh moss mattress. Our bed was kep clean. Much cleaner den de beds of ta-day [sic]. Dey was scrubbed ev'ry Saturday. Dere wasn't a chince [bedbug] on a one of em. Better not see a chince on a bed. De master would sur fuss er bout it. I remember one day another master brought one of his slaves over wid him when he came to see mah master's daughter. And de fust thing mah master wanted to know was did dat darky have any fleas, bugs or chinces on him. All de beds was made by carpenters on de plantation. Dere was fo rows of houses for de quarters. Dere was no paint on dem, also had a house fo children and a hospital. Grandma Delaite had charge of de hospital. No in deed mah master didn't want no children to wurk. He used ta say all de time, don't let dem little darkies wurk. It might hurt dem and dere is enough of dem older darkies on dis farm fo wurk. An listen dere was two nurses in de hospital to tak care of de children. Dere mudders did not have time to tak care of dem. All de master wanted was fo dem wimmen to have children. Dey receive de best of fud [food] an attention. A hog was killed ev'ryday fo dem children. Ise knows case [because] I was dere. Ole man Ben did de carving. Ev'rybody salted dere own meat. Thousands of cattle was raised on de plantation.

"I remember eating out of a pan when two drivers came up an told me to stop[,] dat I had enough. Well sir, I told mah mudder and she told mah master and did he raise hell! Dere was two drivers. . . . De drivers' name was Elliot Saunders and Simon. Both was darkies. Elliot was a bright darky and Simon was black. Dey wasn't zactly mean but dey would whip ya when ya did something bad. Ise don't know whar dem darkies com from but dey must er been free darkies case de master took dem to France one time.

"One day Simon went looking fo a darky name Jim who had run away. Old Jim used to run away all de time. He got his whipping too. De drivers would tak turns on him, even tied him to a tree . . . but dat didn't do [no] gud. Dey jest got tired whipping Jim. Anyhow, Simon went lookin' fo Jim. He looked an looked and all of a sudden he came upon Jim hiding behind a tree. Jim squatted when he saw Simon an' Simon pulled a gun when he saw Jim but dat didn't do any gud case Jim hid and couldn't be seen. Simon looked agin but couldn't find Jim. He looked all over de woods den he saw Jim agin. He fired 'bang'. He fired 'bang'. Well sir, he went whar Jim was but Jim was not dere. He looked an looked agin but could not find Jim. Simon got tired looking, he didn't know what to do. He thought dat he had killed Jim and came on back home. He told ev'rybody, 'Well, I got runaway Jim at last. De old darky is dead, yeah, he is dead'. Ev'rybody felt sorry fo Jim. He was a gud fellow. Only tried to git freedom. Ya can't blame a man case he trys to git freedom. Can ya? Dere was er moanin' an er cryin' all over de plantation an finally master heahed [heard] er bout it. He says, 'What is all dis cryin' bout Jim. You darkies act lak Jim is im'potant. He aint de only big and gud man on dis farm. Now git back to wurk an fo'git about Jim'. But de darkies prayed at night tryin' ta keep Jim's soul out of hell. We jest knew dat he was foolin' wid de debbil. Old Jim would fool wid anybody. After all de fuss, prayers and ev'rything was over up popped Jim to git something to eat. He posed as a preacher off a nearby farm. A feller name Jack was de fust one to see him. Jack ran hollerin' all over de place dat Jim had com back to life. People was nearly crazy. Nebber headed of a man, cep Gawd, comin back ta life. Well sir, heheheh [laughs], Jim had done com back ta life. De darkies nearly had a holiday. Mah master wasn't dere. He had gone away wid his family. De two drivers heahed er bout it but was fraid to com near Jim. Dey was scared stiff. All de darkies went runnin' to Jim askin him er bout hebbin [heaven]. Jim tol' 'em dat hebbin was a gud place. Dat St. Peter was glad to see him[,] tol' him to walk straight to de master an say to let all of his people free. Jim says too, 'St. Peter says "welcome, Jim. Howya." Ise says "Hello St. Peter, I um a gud man livin on Master Landro's farm." He was surprised, sayin "a gud man lak yu a slave. Boy, go down on earth an tell dat master if he don't let yu an all dem darkies go I um comin down mah self." No, I didn't see Gawd. He was too busy. Nebber seen a man so busy. Guess its caise [because] dere is too many people lak Elliot, Simon, and de master on earth. Whar is Simon?' Well sir, de darkies had Jim b'leivin dat he was really dead an' had com back to earth. Old Jim braced up an got big, stuck his shoulders out and pouted, 'Ise gwine to start a mess round heah.' He looked fo Simon. He looked fo Elliot. Nobody could be found. All de darkies was reddy to go wid Jim. Dey refuse to wurk fo anybody caise Jim had tol' dem not to wurk. An den de master came back. He says 'send me dat man dat jest came from hebbin.' Old Jim took one of de master's tuxedo suit. He was a dressed up darky. Ev'rybody went looking ta see what was gwine to happen, if St. Peter was gwine to help Jim. Dere was a holiday. Nobody wurked. Mah master's family sat on de front porch waiting fo Jim. After er while Jim stepped on de front porch an mah master says 'Jim, dey tell me dat ya went to hebbin.' Jim answered, 'Yas master Ise did an St. Peter tol' me to tell ya to let de people go free.' 'Now Jim, don't tell me what St. Peter said caise I aint thinkin er bout him.' Old Jim's eyes got as big as an apple. He rolled dem eyes er round at de people an looked scared stiff, 'Master, ya mean ya aint er fraid of St. Peter?' 'No, not at all Jim. I aint got no love in mah heart fo St. Peter an I nebber will hav any. Did ya see anybody else? Dey tell me dat ya was far away from Gawd. In fact, he was too busy ta see ya. Well Jim if ya didn't see Gawd ya didn't see anybody as far as I um concerned.' Jim started to run. Old master grabbed his shot gun an says 'dis is one time ya will either go to hell or hebbin Jim if ya run.' De people looked at Jim an dey looked at de master. Jim was foolin but de master wasn't foolin. Jim had ta confess. He says, 'Old master got me at last.' Master was mean ta him. He tol' Jim to go back ta wurk an nebber run away agin.

"Mah mudder was a house maid. She got no money. No, I was old enough ta work. Dont know how old I was. I was er bout to pick peas in de pea patch right in front of de house when de war came. See dis mark (a scar on her left arm), Jim Patrick did it. Yeah de sam Jim dat tried to run away.

"Mah mudder planted corn but de master bought it

from her. He paid fifty cents per barrel for corn. Mah mudder bought good clothes wid de money, nothing but silk dresses. Mah children went ta school in dem dresses. Nebber did sav money. We use to play wid it.

"Sure we ate gud food. Drank plenty of milk, clabber [curdled milk], and ate gud bread. Ev'rything was made on de plantation by plantation people. Mah father caught possum but I didn't lak possum. He went out at night trapping but de drivers didn't know it. No sir, he wasn't allowed to go out at night but would steal out. De quarters had cat holes for cats to come in an out. When we ate possum we would stop up de holes to keep de scent from leakin' out. Ya got a whippin if de scent got out. We ate plenty of rabbits, ate fish an ev'rything the master ate. De master would ask, 'Did dem darkies git gud fud?' Ise laked [liked] gud meat best, especially spare ribs an chicken. Talkin er bout garden. Shucks yu aint seen no garden. We had a garden right in front of our quarter. We planted ev'rything in it. Had watermelon, mushmelon, and a flower garden.

"De slaves wore plain ruf lined [*sic*] dresses, yellow cotton dresses in hot weather. Old lady Betsy Adams was de seamstress. I use to liv wid her. She died since de war. De slaves had de best of shoes too. De master brought his house people shoes from France. Dey had to look gud, caise de master had plenty of company. Dere was a big brick house fo de shoemaker shop. De shoemaker was cullored. He was free. His name was Beverly. He tanned the hides and did ev'rything. Even teached de darkies, dat is, de young ones. De slaves wore thick yarn clothes in winter. Winter clothes was made in summer an summer clothes was made in winter.

We sold old clothes to darkies who had mean masters. Dey had to hide 'em though. De slaves dressed up on Sunday. Yeah, de Landro darkies had ev'rything.

"Dere was three cooks fo master Landro. One to boil only. De cooks use to mak all kinds of fancy fud. Miss Zabel, de master's furst cousin who looked white[,] use to teach de cooks all de fancy dishes dat she knew er bout in France. Now dis was a stylish lady an had plenty of money. Another darky dat was kin to master Landro is Joe Brown. Dis was a gud lookin' darky. He had money too but Ise dont know what came of it when de Yankees came. Master had two beautiful daughters. One's name was Marie. I fo'got de other one's name. Mistress Elizabeth, master's wife[,] was beautiful too. Dey didn't hav to use no paint on dere face lak de people do taday. Dey was nut'yu'rally beautiful. I 'member one day de mistress came down to our quarter. She didn't com much but when she came she was lookin prutty. She had black hair an wore silk[,] red, white an blue waist. All de children ran to see her. Nebber did dey see a pusson dressed up lak dat. De mistress jest looked er round.

"Rogers an Abraham Rugless, po white trash, would wait at night to catch de darkies an bring 'em to dey masters. Some of de masters would pay dem fo dis but not mah master. He would run 'em away when dey came ta him wid his people. He would examine dem, too, and tol' dem if anybody would scare or hurt his people dey was in a big humbug wid him. Child, dem po white trash did not fool wid master Landro's people. No sir! Yeahed [*sic*], we called 'em po white trash. Dats all dey was. All dey could do was catch slaves fa money. Dey would whip 'em fo money, too. Dey hated mah master's darkies. Says dey was treated too gud fo niggers. We tol''em we would rather be a nigger den a po white trash. Dat used to mak 'em mad. Mr. Barrow was one gud po white trash who didn't catch slaves at night. He lived in Lafourche Parish.

"De slaves went in a cot [cart] to de field to pick cotton, corn, potatoes and sugar cane. Dey didn't com back fo lunch. It was brought to dem. Dey came home fo' dinner dough [sic]. Dem fools would eat too. Ev'rybody ate in his own quarter.

"Dey slaves was punished fo' fights, being late fo wurk, lying, runnin' away and stealin'. Dey would put ya in a stark [stock]. Yo hands an foots was buckled up an ya stayed dere fo months. No, dey did not hang ya. Nebber heahed of hangin' until taday lak people do. Ya jest got a whippin. Dey gav ya fud when ya was punished. Yas, some of de master was mean but dey did not hang anybody. De mean master would tie de slaves to a tree and beat dem to death.

"Old lady Cater ran away and built a home in de ground. She had six children. De driver caught her one day an whipped her to death. He beat her until her skin fell off an she died. Den he unloosened her from de tree an buried her in de ground in front of de quarters. De drivers used a platted rawhide whip. If he didn't want to hurt ya he would pop de whip and let some of de licks go by. Dis was done to fool de master who headed [heard] de licks inside of de house. I remember one day a gud friend of one of de drivers did something wrong. De driver brought him an tied him to a tree and jest popped de whip. De darky hollered and hollered. He hollered an cried so much dat de master says to let dat darky alone. An de whip ain't nebber teched him.

"No, I ain't nebber seen an auction block but Ise seen slaves when dey jest com off de auction block[.] Dey would be sweatin' and lookin' sick. Some of 'em looked all right but most of 'em was tired lookin'. Dey traveled on ships. Slaves was sold on Napoleon Avenue. Yeahed [*sic*] dere was a special quarter on de ship fo slaves. Yeah, Ise saw slaves in chains. Ise seen 'em wurk in chains. Dey pinned chains er round ya ankle when ya tried ta run away.

"Mah master brought er cullored man, John Adams, from France to teach us how to pray, read and write. We went to his house. He lived in a big house lak de houses on St. Charles Avenue. Yeahed [*sic*] he lived on de plantation. But we had our own chirch in de brick yard way out on de field. We hid behind de brick an had chirch ev'ry night. We was only supposed to have chirch on Sunday but we wanted ta pray all of de time. Old man Mingo preached an dere was Bible lessons. Mingo's famous text was 'Pure gold tried by de fire.' He gave sacraments in a cup. Mah master didn't wan' us to hav too much religion caise de darkies would giv him all religion an' no work. Den, too, he says dat we stayed up too late singing and so could not do a gud day's work de next day; but we hid an prayed jest de same. No sir, nothing could stop us from prayin to Gawd. We didn't use light. We prayed in de dark, children an all. Sometimes we would put grease in a can an burn it. De preacher had to sit over de can to read his Bible. One time de preacher caught on fire. Dere was some screaming. One of the drivers caught us an de master whipped all dem dat was late fo wurk de next day.

Yeah, we sang spirituals. Mah favorite one was 'Better Mind How You Walk On De Cross.' Yeah, we shouted all night. Chirch lasted all night an way into de mornin'. Dis is de way 'Better Mind How You Walk On De Cross' goes:

> Better mind how you talk on de cross
> Better mind how you talk on de cross
> Ya foot might slip an ya soul get lost
> Better mind how you walk on de cross
> Better mind how you walk on de cross
> How ya walk an talk er bout Jesus
> How ya lean, walk on, talk er bout de cross
> Better mind how ya walk on de cross
> How ya walk on de cross, walk on de cross
> I um leanin on Jesus, leanin on Jesus
> Better mind how ya walk on de cross.

"We got happy when dat hymn was sung. De darkies would sing an ya ought er heahed [heard] dem. De old preacher would stomp his foots an all de people would pray an shout. Yeah, we had those good baptisms in a pond whar dey drew water for the sugar house. Dere was baptisms sometime once, twice an three per year as de situation called for. Yeah, ev'body was anxious to git baptized to sav dere soul. It was a deep pond whar dey would git baptize, too. De preacher would say: 'Halleluah, Halleluah!' We sang dis hymn:

> I baptize yo in de ribber Jordan
> I baptize yo in de ribber Jordan
> Halleluah, Halleluah, Halleluah, Lord.

Children, com er runnin', com er runnin'
I baptize yo in de ribber Jordan
I baptize yo in de ribber Jordan
Children, com er runnin', com er runnin'.

"De preacher would say, 'I baptize yo in de name of de Father, Son an de Holy Ghost.' I remember one day an old lady wanted religion so bad dat she tol' de preacher dat she was anxious to git to hebbin and was cryin' 'Lord, sav me.' De preacher went er runnin' an hollerin'. He said, 'Sister, I um gonna sav yo but ya got to prove it to de Lord! Prove dat ya is in a position to be saved.' Well sir, ev'rybody checked dis old gal an found her ta be one of the biggest rascals on de plantation. Sich a big rascal dat de men didn't want her. She was too big a jackass an' too big a witch. No, I dunno nothin er bout hoodoo. Nebber heahed er bout dat stuff until I came heah. Dere was mo religious wimmen den men. De preacher didn't receive no money. He wurked on de plantation lak ev'rybody else. Dat went fo all preachers, unless it was somebody dat master brought from France. We didn't lak to go to anybody brought from France caise ya could not do lak ya wanted to do. Ya could not be free to shout. Gawd says dat ya must shout if ya want to be saved. Dats in de Bible. Don't ya know it?

"Funerals? All of de slaves was buried in swell looking coffins, well made, too. Dey was covered with white cotton. No children would play er round de place whar de coffin was made. Yeah, all de coffins was made on de plantation by hand. Yeah, free men made dem. De dead folks had de best preacher on de plantation. His name was Reverend Jacob

Nelson. He spoke French, English, Latin, Greek, and Spanish. He was a slave jest caise he was too smart. Mah master was er fraid dat he would teach de slaves something he didn't want dem ta know, dats why he was a slave. He was brought heah a free man but made a slave when he refused to obey de master. Master Landro would not let him go back to France. De edumoncated [*sic*] white folks came to heah dis man preach. Oh! dat man could preach. He went er growlin', cryin' from de heart an talkin' in all dose many languages dat de people didn't know anything er bout an de crowd went wild, most of dem fainted. De slaves went to de funeral in carriages. De white folks went in dere large wagons with slave drivers. It was lak a picnic when a slave would die an Reverend Nelson would preach de funeral. De funeral song dat I lak best was:

> Out from de tomb a doanful [*sic*] sound
> Out from de tomb a doanful sound
> And I heahed a tender cry
> Out from de tomb a doanful sound
> A livin' man came [and] viewed de ground
> Of every sinful heart, of every sinful heart.

"Dat is de only one dat Ise remember. No, we did not sing 'Nearer Mah Gawd To Thee'. Heah is another hymn we sang in slavery:

> Oh whar is He, Oh whar is He
> Born de King of Jews?
> Oh whar is He wid dat gud news?
> May Jesus wash mah sins er way.

Born de king of Jews?
Oh whar is He wid dat gud news?
Oh whar is He born de king of Jews?
I um standin on de ladder washing mah sins er
  way
I um standin heah wid a heart dat will stay
Waitin' fo mah Lord, oh whar is He born de king
  of Jews?
Oh whar is He wid dat gud news an born de king
  of Jews?

"Mah master . . . use to tell us dat de Yankees was er comin someday but would not kill him. I saw him tak his money away with him. Yeah, slaves ran away up north, sayin dat de people up dere was treatin people lak dey was human beings an not lak dey was dogs. Yeah, some of de masters was very mean an whipped an did not feed dey slaves. I know a woman who was a slave. She said dat her master was so mean dat he died wid his eyes wide open. Whenever ya see a man die wid his eyes wide open he is a dirty rascal an mean to people. Many slaves stold [*sic*] away an went up north. Dey was stealin an runnin away ev'ryday. Dey would hide on de ships, swim an do ev'rything to git er way.

"All masters had differ'rent laws. I nebber heahed nuthin about patrollers. . . . News? We carried news by stealin off. Shucks, we knew ev'rything de master talked er bout. De house girl would tell us an we would pass it er round. Dats how we knew dat master was afraid of de yankees. Mah mudder says dat one day she heahed master say dat de yankees would kill dem an tak all de slaves an free dem. How did we steal off? Through chicken holes. De slaves had balls in de sugar house. Dey would start late an was way out in de field whar de master could not heah dem. Not a bit of noise could be heahed. No sir, de slaves had some swell times. In case ya was caught, ya was whipped. Dey danced by candle light. Dey got back in dere quarters fo daylight. Ya could not look to[o] tired de next day, neither. If ya did de furst thing de driver would say was dat ya was out last night en den de whippin would follow. Dese songs was sung:

> Whip er wop, whip er wop youee
> We gonna sing and dance an sing
> Whip er wop, whip er wop youee
> Singin, singin an dancin' youee
> Dancin, singin' an dancin' youee
> Whip er wop, whip er wop youee.

"De slaves could dance too. Dey did de buck dance and de shimmie. Dey would dance lak dis. (Two steps to the right and two to the left.) Den dey would shake dere skirts an de men would dance er round dem; we would do dis (the dance that Mrs. Hite demonstrated is very much like the Scottische). When master's daughter had company of white folks from France or up north he would git his darkies an giv' em liquor to dance. De darkies would git in front of de house an dance down to de bricks. Master an his white folks friends would jest laugh an giv de darkies liquor. Dey would mak music wid pans, beat on pots wid sticks an sing. Whenever dere was a contest a man named Jolly would win all of 'em. Dis darky sur could dance. Boy, when he started twirling his legs an stickin out his back old master would holler.

Wouldn't let Jolly wurk hard either. Caise he was de best dat master Landro had. He won plenty of money dancin fo master. Master says he was gwine to tak Jolly to France but de mistress wouldn't let him. She use to always say dat Jolly was her fav'errite joy. Jolly was a tall fellow, skinny, wid long legs an a peanut lookin' head. He was black wid pearly white teeth. He had big feet too. Yeah, Jolly was a disfigured man. But master would fight for him. I'll nebber fo'git all de humbug dat he cause one day when he took a stroll from de place dat he an Master Landro went to. Ya see, master took Jolly to a plantation to dance against a slave of one of his friends. Jolly beat de man dancin'. Fo ya know it, he had done been in de man's house makin lov to de man's wife in de man's bed. Dere was a big fight. Jolly knocked de man out cold. Bein' by himself all de slaves jumped on Jolly an beat him up. Master heahed er bout it an brought Jolly back an made him fight al[l] de slaves one by one. Jolly beat dem all up an master Landro helped him while his friend jest sat dere. He had batter [*sic*] jest sat dere caise master Landro was a gud man. Dat was de time dat he wanted to carry Jolly to France but Mistress says 'no indeed, dis Jolly is ma pride an joy.'

"Some of de slaves was bad. Dey would beat up de master an his family. Some of dem would kill dere master but not on our plantation. [O]h yeah, jest once. A man name John beat up master one day but master got de best of him when he rested. Dis day master went on de field to inspect things. John was er foolin er round. He was lazy anyhow. Ya know one of dese smart fellows who tries to put all de wurk on de other fellow. Master caught John in de act an popped him on de eye. All of a sudden John cracked master side de head, an fo ya know it he was down on de ground. Mah mudder was right dere. She says dat master got up an John popped him agin. Dis time master stayed down. De drivers rushed to kill John but master says 'no, I will tak care of him after dinner.' Master went in an had a good rest. After dinner he came back lookin fo John. John saw him comin an ran. Master says dat he was gwine to giv him a chance to do dat agin. He squared off at John an wid one blow John was on de ground an stayed dere. Dey had to git de doctor fo John. We use to heah er bout de slaves dat beat up dere masters an runnin er way. Wished I had de dollars fo de slaves dat beat up dere masters. I would be rich. Mah grandfather Edmond Louis beat up his master something terrible. De master laked him so much dat he wouldn't whip him. Mah grandfather was de coachman but after he whipped de master dey put him in de corn field. He says dat he had nebber seen a corn field. But when dey put him in line an tol' him he better be de furst one finish ev'rytime mah grandfather says he would. I um telling ya dat he was de furst one to finish an asked fo mo.

"De slaves had a gud time in dere quarters. Dey played guitar, danced fo de light went out. Dey put skin over a barrel fo a drum. Dey talked er bout de master's business in dere quarters too.

"De slave[s] wurked on Sunday and Saturday sometimes. Most of de time dey didn't. De Sunday wurk was light. Dey would only pull shucks of corn. De corn shucks was given to de cows. On big holidays de slaves didn't wurk. On Christmas master would giv his slaves presents. Dey would be clothes most of de time. I don't remember wurkin on New Years Day.

"De children shot marbles an played games[.] All children were christened at eight years ole in de Catholic church. De wimmen gambled in de woods playin cards an dice. Yeah, de children played games, dey played Yankee Doodle Dandy.

"Yeah, Ise seen a witch. Dey is lak a big turkey wid no eyes. Sometimes dey look lak de debbil wid horns an ev-erything. Ise seen 'em comin in de house over de sill of de door. We use to hollow [holler] when we seen 'em but mah mudder says dat dey don't harm gud children. Yeah a story? No, dis is de truth. One day a witch picked up a woman an carried her off an nobody knows whar she is at. De master an all de drivers looked fo de woman but nobody could find her. De witch took er away. People use to tell her dat was gwine to happen caise she was a bad woman who 'fuse [re-fused] to go to chirch. I had dat heartfelt religion an prayed to Gawd to hold ma mind in his hand.

"Sometime de slaves would hav marriages lak de peo-ple do today wid all de same trimmings. De veil, gown an ev'rything. Dey married fo de preacher an had big affairs in dere quarters. Den sometime dey would go to de master to git his permission an blessings an he would say, 'C'mon darky jump over dis brum an call yo' self man an wife.' Mas-ter might er gav some of dem darkies present or sumpin caise dere was er lot of darkies gwine to master. Shucks[,] some of dem darkies didn't care er bout master, preacher or nobody[,] dey jest went an got married, married demselves. Don't know how dey did it but dey did it dough [*sic*]!

"Tell a story dat I heahed? Well, mah nervous condition kind er keep me from rememberin' ev'rything dat I heahed or know er bout but I do know dis an its de truth. . . . [D]ey tell me:

"Dere was a rabbit an a bear who was in a grocery business. De rabbit was tryin to cheat de bear an de bear was tryin to cheat de rabbit. Dey got er long fin' until one day de rabbit's friend tol him dat de bear was crooked an de bear's friends tol' him dat de rabbit was crooked. De only way to tell if someone is crooked is to try ya wife on 'em[,] both of dem thought. Well, sir, de bear sent his wife in an de rabbit sent his wife in de grocery store. De bear made lov to de rabbit's wife and de rabbit made lov to de bear's wife. Neither one knew er bout [the other]. One day de bear's wife tol him what a nice man de rabbit was. De bear says, 'well, well I caught him at last. Any time a man will make lov to ya wife he will steal ya groceries.' Mrs. bear says 'yeah ya caught him at last. He made lov ta me.' De bear went runnin out of de house lookin fo de rabbit. Well sir, de rabbit was talkin to his wife. He says what a nice man de bear was an his wife says 'he fooled you caise he made lov ta me.' So, he figured anytime a man will mak lov to ya wife he will steal ya groceries. So, de rabbit left his house lookin fo de bear. And lo it all! Dey met in de center of de road. Both hollered out loud dat his wife an groceries had been molested. Upon learnin dat both wives had been made lov to and dat an equal number of groceries was stolen by each dey shook hands and says dat it is gud ta know dat dere is mo den one thief in de world.

"Did ya heah er bout de smart darky dat a master had? Dis darky could guess anything in de world. So, his master figured dat he could make money off of him. He took dis old darky er round his friends an bet dat he could guess anything dat dey was thinking er bout. De old darky won de bets from his master's friends an made his master rich. So, one day a man came down from de north wid plenty of money lookin fo dis darky who was so smart an could guess ev'rything people was thinkin er bout or could wurk out problems. He bet the master one thousand dollars dat he would get something dat de darky couldn't guess and giv him three times to guess it. De man from de north came up wid something in a box. He says 'guess, darky, Ise gwin to giv three guesses.' De darky's master an mistress was jest er pullin fo him[,] sayin 'comon [come on], guess des [this] an we is all rich.' De old darky took one guess. He says 'ya got a rabbit in dat box.' De man from de north laughed and says 'I got dis darky now.' De darky looked at his boss an winked, foolin his boss. De master really thought dat de old darky was knowin what he was doin. De darky took another guess. Dis time he says 'ya got a shot gun in dat box.' De man from de north shook his head an laughed out loud, 'no indeed, you is wrong.' De old darky took a look at his boss an shook his head. . . . His master an mistress commence gettin worried. Dey looked at him while he was wonderin'. Finally, de old darky looked at his boss and said, '*DEY CAUGHT DE OLD COON AT LAST*.' De man from de north says 'I'll be damn! Dat's what it is[,] a coon. Tak de money.' Ev'rybody hugged de old darky.

"De slaves might er did hoodoo but I nebber heahed nuthin er bout it until I came heah. Ise knows de people heah do hoodoo wurk caise some of dem com to me caise dey know I um old an figure dat Ise know something er bout it, but I don't know er thing.

"De slaves got de best of attention. Two white doctors, Stone an Baillet[,] served dem. No sir, master Landro was makin too much money off of his darkies to let 'em die lak mules. Dey was gud workers.

"Freedom had been given long fo we knew anything er bout it. Master Landro and de driver would not tell us. Dey tried an tried to keep us as slaves. Mah mudder says dat Elliot and Simon was beat up. A fellow name Benjamin came on our plantation an hung up de American flag on a freedom poll [sic]. Ev'rybody ran into de streets hollorin' 'we is free at last.' De yankees shook our hands, dere was singin, prayin an ev'rythin. De yankees beat up all dose masters who refused to let de slaves go when dey was supposed to. Our master ran away to France. Abraham Lincoln came and tol ev'rybody dat dey was gwin to git free schools. He talked to us from a gun boat on de ribber. He says dat he was cumin back but nebber did. All de big folks had gone; dere was nothing heah but de little folks. Dey gav us land but some of de po white trash took it away from de slaves. Dere was killin an fightin after de yankees left. De slaves lost most of de battles caise some of de men had big guns. A lot of dem came from Texas an other hiding places after de yankees left. Dey was scared stiff of de yankees.

"De slaves went to farmin after freedom. Dey sold dere crops to de white men an went to school. White people teached de school. Dere was religious people tryin to git de slaves to go to chirch but some kind of riders came along an tol dem dat dey must not teach niggers. I heahed of de Ku Klux Klans in Texas. Dey didn't com whar I lived. Dese riders didn't wear anything over dere faces or heads. Dey was jest lak ev'ryday people. Dey was nothin but de po white trash. Dese was de people who had nothin.

"I heahed er bout Booker T. Washington. I b'lieve dat all cullored people must be edumoncated [*sic*] an lov one another an be religious. Taday if a man got plenty of money he is looked upon. Ise prayin fo de world to be saved. I use ta wurk fo A. C. Littlejohn who is kin to Jefferson Davis.

"Mah mudder was robbed by po white trash in Napoleonville. She had $1200.00 worth of property taken away from her dere. De government men tol her she would git it back but she nebber did. Mah mudder died on a Saturday night. $1000.00 had jest com from Washington fo her but we had to send it back.

"Mah husband made gud money farmin. We bought furniture for $300.00. Did not live lak rats. We lived gud. I made gud money wurkin for Mrs. Littlejohn. She put me heah but she is dead now, I guess[,] an I um all alone. I wish de government would do somethin fo me. Can't ya help me to git something?"

ODEL JACKSON

Age: 81
1233 Nunez Street, Algiers
May 31, 1940

"I's been here in Algiers for 51 years, was born in La Fuche [Lafourche] parish December 17, 1858. Mother of 16 children, ten dead and six a-living. My ma and her older childs was brought from Virginia and sold at the French market, and taken to La Fouche [*sic*] parish, and dat's where I come into de world. I don't have no good rememberance [*sic*], very few things dat I can think of. I do knows when I was small my ma had a hard time working. De ole Missus was mean[,] would tie her and beat her most to death. After us was sat [*sic*] free we most starved to death. I would slip around and eat out of people's slop cans. I would be so hungry. My pa cooked for some of de sojers. My oldest brother would take something to eat to de mens at Fort Hudson. One day de Yankee sojers captured him, us never did see him any more. After us was free Pa and Ma only got 30¢ and 15¢ a day for a long time for dare work. I never is went to school, was christen Catholic, but I's Baptist now. We never was allowed any time off for anything. . . .

"I got married when I was fifteen years old. Me and my ole man never did git along together. We was always fiting [fighting] and fiting. He would jump on me in de cain [*sic*] fields and beat me up or cut me with de cain knives.

"He was a no good man, I run away and married him, so I decided to stay with him, if we were fiting all time. He got to running around with a ole 'oman. She got all his money. All I ever got was a beating and babies. Stayed with him until I got through breeding. I know one time I was in de bed with one of de babies, and his 'oman come in and hoodooed me. I heard her when she was opening the door. I calls my ma and she did not answer me, she had done gone to sleep. De lamp was burning low. . . . Dat ole 'oman come in, I screamed and tried to wake my Ma, she had a little lamp in her hand, she grabbed my knee.

"It hurt me so until I couldn't move it. I screamed again and my Ma woke. I asked her did she see dat 'oman in there, she says 'No you are just dreaming.' De door was open, the ole hussie did not take time to close it. You know, Miss, dat 'oman put a snake in my leg. I's still cripple yet. You know my leg was so bad until I could not walk for a long time, finally I got a root Dr. to do something for my leg. But it still bothers me yet. Dat been 40 years ago[. D]at snake would just crawl and knot up in my leg, so's finally he got it kilt.

"After that she come back to beg apoligese [*sic*], but it was too late then, I was already cripple den.

"Worked around white folks all my life, cooking, sewing, and washing. I did ever'thing I could to make a living for my chaps. I's too ole to work now. But de Lords [*sic*] has been good to me. I thank him for my bread now, you know miss, I never did smoke or dance, drink, go to the shows or nothing like dat. I seed a little boy past yesterday smoking. It make me think of a little verse I usto [*sic*] say all time.

> Robert Reed was only ten years old
> And he never smoked or chewed.
> 'It's a filthy weed,' says Robert Reed,
> 'And hurts the health and makes bad breath.'
> There is idle Jerry Jones, He smokes
> And him only ten years old, and thot [*sic*]
> It made him big,
> And set behind the cabin door."

DAFFNEY JOHNSON

Age: 90
518 Robinson Avenue, Marrero
July 16, 1940

"I's around 90 yrs old[,] don't no zackly, dey got my age down dare in Gretna. Don't remember very much. Done got to[o] old to think. Was borned on Miller Don plantation.

"Wuz a slave during my childhood[.] Maw's name Di-anna, pa's name wuz Isaac Johnson, I had five sisters and four brothers.

"When I was young I had to mind de chillin, jest as soon as I got big enough de Boss put me in de cain [*sic*] fields. My old Missus just died a few years ago, she stayed over in de city. We had a colored driver, he sho did push us out in dem sugar cain [*sic*] fields. I never did get a beating[. D]ey had a [w]hole bunch of cats and when dey punished us dey would have our back stripped and make de cat mad and let em scratch de blood out of our backs. Dat was the way us was beat.

"We all'us had plenty to eat sich as it was. Grits[,] Cornmeal & Meat[,] it was all raised on de plantation. I's

Baptist. My pa and maw never did marry like de people do now daze.

"I is de mother of eight children myself[. A]ll of dem is dead but one, my misses name was Miss Taylor. I worked around de house a long time fo [before] de boss put me in de sugar cain [*sic*] fields. I noes one time when I was small us all had what dey called the seven year itch, de ole Miss'us made my maw dig a pot of poke root and hide it and put us chaps in it. If us had been put in de fire we would not have burned any worse but it sho did cure dat itch.

"Us never did no what it was to play going fishing are [or] any thing like that.

"Sometimes dey would let us go to church[. N]ever could read nor write[,] de white folks did not allow dat.

"Never will forget de day us was sat [*sic*] free. How dey fired de big gun. Us stayed right on with de ole Boss & Missus for a long time after us was sat [*sic*] free. He paid us off ever Saturday. For our work if a woman made two bits a day dat was good money[. U]s never did no what money was for until us was sat [*sic*] free[. D]en us did not no how to spend it.

"I sho is glad dat dem daze is over now.

"My maw and pa did not no where to go so de boss said dey could stay dare . . . and he would feed us on and pay us wages for working.

"You jest have to call another day[,] den maybe I can get my mind together."

HANNAH KELLY

Age: unknown
503 Wyer Street, Gretna
Interviewer: Flossie McElwee

"I was born in Louisville, Kentucky. During the war I was [a] refugee to Texas. Our Missus brung us to Texas. I was ten years ole when peace declared.

"My Missus was Lou Downward. I never did do any work, only nurse the children during slavery.

"I had six brothers and one sister. My ma worked in the spinning and weaving, and making dyes. She would take shu-make [sumac] berries and make red, Black Jack made a brown dye & etcs. De boys dey worked in [the] fields, after us was brung to Texas. The boys worked in de fields raised cotton, corn, 'taters.

"We had meat, bread, vegetables, sometimes on Sunday or a holiday we would have biscuit.

"I can't say dat de old Madam was not good to us, for she always was, can't even remember her having us whipped, you see my Ma worked all [the] time making cloth. She was real good at that, we allus had good clothes and shoes. I can't say anything about my owner.

"My Ma was borned in Virgin[i]a. My Pa in Kentucky. Hannah Weather was my Ma, my pa's name Reuben. Us lived in log cabins. We allus had good beds and enough quilts in winter time to be warm.

"She [the mistress] even raised my Ma and den us. I knows when it use to rain she would put all de mens in the crib shucking corn; too wet to plow. She had dem cutting wood. She never did have any trouble with her niggers. I knows they use to whip dem awful at the next plantation. We come thru here when us was on our way to Texas. When us stopped it was at Madisonville. Never did learn to read nor write, didn't know what church was until peace. My Missus brother was a Doctor. He always give us medecine [*sic*] when us was sick.

"Oh yes! We didn't do like dis young generation. We had certain times to go to bed and three o'clock to be up. The boys sometimes would get to go to parties, but we never did. They checked dem out and when dey come in.

"We never did work on Sunday like some people say dey did. Our Missus knew we were gwine be free, she told my Ma we could go or stay, so we left soon after peace [was] declared. Us was sat [*sic*] free the 19th of June. Dat day useto [*sic*] be celebrated in Texas. She went to Mulgan [?], Texas. Taken in washing and ironing, did all kinds of house work for a very little pay. So when de yellow fever broke out, my Ma and all de rest died with it. I married in Texas befo' I come to Louisiana, had a church wedding. I's Methodist. I's de Mother of de church here in Gretna. I's de oldest one in de church. Tell you Miss, people nowadays didn't have to do like I did. I have worked all my life. I prays every nite that our people will stay out of the War [World War II]. I lived to see three wars already. I never believed in spirits or things like that."

FRANCES LEWIS

Age: 86
1042 General Taylor Avenue

Born a slave, in Georgia, 86 years ago, Frances' wooly head, broad features and coal black skin tell you that she is proud of the fact that she is a genuine old-fashioned "cullud woman with good raisin'."

This is what she tells:

"I was just about eleven years of age, when Sherman's Brigade went marchin' through Georgia. It looked like a million men an' maybe there was that many, I don't know.

"The sojers wore blue jackets with brass buttons, an' there was dead an' dyin' all over the roads and the fiel's, ev'rywhere you went you saw them an' blood was jes' a runnin'.

"The sojers sang 'Yankee Doodle Dander' but I don' see how they could sing or have music when dead was all aroun'. Husban's an' fathers an' sons gone from they loved ones. Maybe they were jes' tryin' to keep up courage.

"Ole Mis' knew them Yankees would steal her silver so she trusted my ma with it, an' my ma hid it good, but when them Yankees came to our house an' axed my ma ef she had anythin' hid my ma tole a story an' sed 'No,' she didn't have ennythin', but they didn't believe her an' they searched the house an' foun' it. But because she wus a slave they didn't do nothin' to her, jes' took the silver.

"An' once I wus sont with Massa's son, a boy 'bout my age[,] to gather ches'nuts, an' when one nice big one fell to the groun' we both run to get it. But I got it fust an' he hit me for it, an' I picked up a stone an' throwed it at him an' it cut a deep hole in his head an' I was scared. My ma whipped me hard, but ole Massa said I'd been punished enough—but I've always been sorry I done it.

"Yes'm I remember old religious himes [hymns] they used to sing but they don't sing 'em [now]. They'd think you were crazy if you did. Did you ever hear this un?

> O Sister Mary, who's on the Lord's side?
> Mary wept an' Martha mourned:
> Who's on the Lord's side?
> I let you know befo' I go who's on the Lord's side. . . .

"There's another one lik' this:

> Roll, Jordan roll,
> Wish I had been there to hear sweet Jordan roll.
> Look over yonder, see what I see,
> A band of Angels comin' after me.
> Roll, Jordan roll, you oughter been there
> To see sweet Jordan roll.
> Roll Jordan roll, you oughter been sittin' in the kingdom
> To hear sweet Jordan roll. . . .

"An' when a sinner got converted, She uster sing while about to shout:

> You may hol' my hat
> You may hol' my shawl,
> But pray don' tech my waterfall. . . .

"Ef people would worship the Lord more the world would be better. Lots of em, white folks too, don' even say grace but jus' gobble they food. On New Year's eve, the horses an' cows an' sheep an' all animals ben' they knees an' lie down in rev'rence to they Creator. Look at the horse when he drinks water, he lif's up he's head as in gratitude. An' the chickens, too."

An' [*sic*] then Frances explained that when she was young, negroes wore what was known as a waterfall. They were made of real hair and had a thin wire to hold them on her head. They were expensive, too, she said[,] and that is why negroes were very careful with them. When they got religion, they shouted, and swooned and fainted and had to be revived. Sometimes it took several persons to hold them. They actually sang the "Waterfall" song given above.

We looked it up in the dictionary and this is how Mr. Webster defines it: "A chignon [hairstyle] likened to a waterfall."

"Ole Miss was good to us. She taught us our ABC's—an' we studied the Blueback [*sic*] Webster an' the McGuffy readin' book—an' to count up to a hundred. That's all the learnin' I ever had. An' she taught us outen a kitycasm [catechism], it was a Sunday-school book, an' I remember some of the questions were:

" 'Who made you?'

"An' we had to say,

" 'God made me an' all mankin'.' And there was lots more questions like that, but I forget what they were. It was on Sunday that we learned this and after that we went to Church.

"We ate in the kitchen at the Big House—all the chil'ren from the quarters—not the big kitchen, but one for us. An' sometimes ole Miss would come in to see that we were properly fed. We had hominy small, they call it grits, now, an' plenty milk to eat on it an' coh'n [corn] bread. That was our breakfus'. At 12 o'clock we had lye or big hominy an' coh'n bread an' pot licker an' collard greens. At night hoe-cake an' buttermilk. On Sunday we had flour bread.

"An' whenever we came in Ole Miss' presence, we curt-sied low an' the boys bowed their heads an' bended one knee. Ef a chile saw this done now they'd think he was crazy.

"I got *Mother wit* [native wit; common sense] instead of an edycation. Lots of colored people in offices an' school don' seem to know what Mother wit is."

As we did not know either, we asked her to tell us just what is was:

"Well, it's lik' this: I got a wit to teach me what's wrong.

"I got a wit to not make me a mischief-maker.

"I got a wit to keep people's trusts. No one has to tell me not to tell what they say to me in confidence, for I respect what they say, an' I never tell.

"I'm glad I had good raisin'. When chil'ren used to get

a whipping they wus taught to turn 'roun' an' say 'Thank you ma'm for whipping me' an' bow. That was mighty hard to do, but we were never allowed to pout—if we did we got another. An' if we just needed being punished we were put behin' a door an' had to stan' on one foot until we were ready to say we were sorry an' promis' not to do it agin. If we tol' a story our mouths were washed out with a soaped rag.

"At Christmus we hung up our stockings in the big house on nails in the mantelpiece, an' each of us got a stick of candy an' . . . a blue-back spellin'-book, Webster. We greeted every one in the big house with 'Chris'mus gif, Chris'mus gif'—an' we were all happy.

"Befo' dinner there was a big eggnog, an' we all had a glassful. It had whiskey in it, but not enough to make you drunk, an' they sung:

> Chris'mas comes but once a year
> An' everyone mus' have his sheer (share).

"We sed our prayers at night[.] The fust one I ever knew, I say it still[. I]t wus: 'Now I lay me.'"

Yes, we replied that was the prayer we were taught. . . . Bishop Green of the Episcopal Church in Mississippi lived to be nearly 90 and he told us that he said this little prayer which his mother had taught him, every night since [he] was able to talk. When he died it was the last thing he was heard to say:

> Now I lay me down to sleep
> I pray thee Lord, my soul to keep

If I should die before I wake
I pray thee Lord my soul to take
And this I ask for Jesus' sake.
Amen.

[Frances Lewis replied,] "An' you sed it too. Now ain' that nice. Some mothers say they ain' got time to bother with they children's prayers. What are they a coming too [*sic*]?" She sighed.

"We learned to count by taking kernels of corn an' puttin' 'em separately an' sayin'—

William a Trimmeltoe, he's a good fisherman
He has hens, puts 'em in pens
Wire, brier, limber-lock
How many geese are in a flock?
One flew east, one flew west
An' one flew over the cuckoo's nes'.

"An' then we counted the dif'rent pens—1-2-3.

"We used to play—'Ring-round the rosy,' an' 'Light my cane!' an' games lik' that but I didn't have much time to play 'cause I wus too busy ev'ry day but Sat'day—then I didn't have to work. Well, I used to rub ole Mis' an' ol' Mas' feet ev'ry night.

"I never had a doll until after I wus married. Then I bought one. It wus the pruttiest thing you ever did see. I put it in a chair an' looked at it. I wus mos' 'fraid to tetch it.

"An' I had to dry the dishes too—an' bring in kinlin' wood, an' anythin' else they tol' me.

"We got two pairs of shoes a year—a pair of brogans an'

a Sunday pair. But the brogans hurt our feet, an' we'd rather go barefooted.

"We didn't get sick much, but when we did Ole Mis' giv' us blue mass pills, an' hippocac [ipecac] an' sassypariller [sarsaparilla]. She took bark an' made a tea outer it, an' for flux she giv' us sage tea.

"When I wus a girl in the country we didn't have church houses, like they got now. The men took some pos'es [posts] stuck in the groun' an' overhead was a lot of saplins, you know what they are? Little trees, well, they were put with one end with branches one way an' the other end the other, an' covered enough to keep out the sun, but it wouldn't keep out the rain. An' they made seats outer rough planks. They had no backs lik now, but we didn't min', an' church lasted all day—an' the groun' was covered with sawdus'. That's why now, at revival meetin's, they say when you go up for prayers that you 'hit the sawdust trail.'

"Befo' I got converted I went to dances, an' we danced by a fiddle, an' the fiddler kep' time with a song

> Hop light ladies, the cake's all dough
> Don' min' the weather, so the win' don' blow.

"An' they had log-rollin's an' quiltin' bees after the surrender.

"When the logs were cut an' ready for buildin' a cabin, all the frens [friends] pitched in an' helped roll the logs to where the hut was to be put up—an' they had all the hog-meat an' bread an' molasses they could eat. After that they put the hut together an' took dirt an' made a sort of plaster outen hit to fill up the chinks.

"In those days people uster help each other in sickness, in trouble an' ev'ry way, now they too busy with theyselves."

HUNTON LOVE

Age: over 100
2111 Philip Street, New Orleans, Louisiana
Interviewer: Posey
January 8, 1941

When a child, we once asked our Father why it was that nearly all negroes lived to such an old age.

His reply was that while many did, few knew how old they really were and that they just guessed or some one assumed they were such and such an age at some particular time.

This is, no doubt, the case, but as often as it may be over-rated, just as often it is under the stated years.

The subject of our sketch, simply states that he is "somewhere over a hundred"—he has no birthday and can't keep up with the time.

There can be no doubt as to this statement, you are assured when you look at him. While his sight is failing and his steps falter, he goes about independently.

He tells you that he was born at Bayou Lafourche on

the plantation of John Viguerie and that he was 21 when his people mustered arms.

"When ole Marse went to war, he left me overseer of the plantation. Yes'm I did—some of the slaves wouldn't mind and I had to whip 'em. . . . Besides I had to show 'em I was boss, or the plantation would be wrecked.

"O, yes, I was whipped once. It wuz my business to keep all the horses slick and clean. Once when Ole Marse was going to ride his horse he took his han'chief and rubbed it down Brutus' back, an' kase [because] it comed out dirty, I got a lidking [*sic*], but that was the onliest time.

"Once when some slaves were sold they were han'cuffed an' tied behin' an' ol' oak tree. Susan was bought an tol' to follow her new Marster. She wuz jus' about in chile-birth and wouldn't move and when urged, said: 'I won't go! I won't go! I won't.' For that she wuz given 150 lashes.

"Another woman was throwed in a big bed of ants which they had caused to 'semble. She was tied down with heavy weights, so she couldn't budge; she was tortured awfully.

"Sometimes I cried after I went to bed, because of these whippin's. Of course, it neces'ry sometimes, but these overseers, gin'rilly men from the North, wuz brutal.

"We didn't leave the place often. When day's work wuz over, we wuz too tired to do ennythin' but go to sleep—an' besides, we didn't know any outsiders. But if we did go, we had to have a pass or we'd be taken up. They wuz strick in those days.

"I worked in the cane juice place. Big boats stopped at our landin' an' they'd take on maybe 150 barrels of sugar, 400 bbls. [barrels of] molasses at a time, sugar wuz king in those days.

"Injuns? I rem'ber them too. After slavery, I went to their tents. They wuz good an' kind unless you treated 'em bad, then they'd turn on you and nothin' wuz too hard for them to do to you. Some people used to say 'a good Injun is a dead Injun' but they didn't deserve that.

"Yes'm, I went to some of their buryin's. They dug a hole big ernuff an' put him in an' throwed dirt over him. They didn't have no coffin. Then they took han's and marched 'roun' singin' an' hollerin'—Nobody cried."

Danced with a Glass of Water on His Head

"When I wuz young, before I wuz converted I loved to dance all night. I could dance with a glass full of water on my head, an' make bows to my lady pardner an' never let a drop out.

"White folks used to get me to do it and they'd give me $5.00[,] sometimes more.

"Culled [colored] people don' seem to be able to hol' ennythin' on they heads enny mo'—not even a basket of clothes. I wonder if they heads is changed! If I was more stiddy on my feet I could do it now.

"We had nice times frolicing [*sic*].—We sang and danced and drank anisette.

"Ten years after peace, I went to Slidell, La., and worked on the farm of Mme. George Benoit. She raised chickens and turkeys to sell and I was good help.

"O, Lordy, Lordy! how we uster sing:

We'll hang Jeff Davis on a sour apple tree
Hang Jeff Davis on a sour apple tree . . .
As we go marchin' on.

"Would you really have done it?" we asked.

"O, Lordy, no man, we wouldn't a hanged him, but he was a tiger, he was bad 'cause he wanted to keep us in slavery an' that was mean in him."

We asked if he had ever seen a coachwhip snake.

"I've seen lots of 'em. They kin whip you to death. They run up trees so they kin spring down on you an' 'less you kill them they'll beat you to deth. That's why they name 'coach-whip,' they resembles a whip. O, Lordy, I alwus had my knife with me an' when I *saw* one, I cut hit in two.

"Once I heard some men talkin' an' one sed: 'You think money grows on trees;' an' the other one say: 'Hit do, git down that moss an' convert it in to money,' an' I got to thinkin' an' sho' 'nuff, it do grow on trees."

CHARLES PARCANSES

Age: 130
5901 Marais Street, New Orleans, Louisiana
Interviewer: Michinard
June 15, 1940

Charles Parcanses was born in Selma, Alabama, in the year 1810. He came to live in New Orleans in 1872.

When the war broke out between the States, Charlie was very anxious to join the army but was rejected owing to his age.

Parcanses' father was a Cherokee Indian, who died at the age of 150 years. Parcanses helped to build the tracks at Manchac.

Parcanses related the following tale:

When a slave, his boss had made a wager with him that he had another slave who could out-eat Parcanses. The wager was accepted and on a certain day, the two Gargantuas [amiable giant with a capacity for food] met and began the meal. Parcanses ate one yearling, one shoat, one skillet full of birds, and one pan of corn-bread. The other slave ate two yearlings, two shoats, and a bushel of sweet potatoes, and after all had been consumed, said: "Marse, I'se could eat more, but I'se will do with this!"

The master had won the wager.

Thirteen years ago, old man Parcanses became very ill. He was taken to the Charity Hospital. The doctors there said he would not live through the day. The old man rallied, remained at the hospital three weeks and returned home perfectly well. His only infirmity now is rheumatism in one knee.

Parcanses admitted he had been a terror in his youth, liking to drink, smoke, and of all, the girls.

"You see," he said to me, with a twinkle of the eyes, "You see, I'se come from a woman so I'se had to go back to them. It's been eight years since I'se gone out with a girl." As he said that the old man chuckled.

GRACIE STAFFORD

Age: unknown
4613 Camp Street, New Orleans, Louisiana
Interviewer: Posey
October 23, 1940

In the next house but one from Mary Harris [see page 173], lives another ex-slave Gracie Stafford. Their experiences in life are similar and they are devoted and congenial friends.

Our subject, as she tells it was born on the Myrtle Grove Plantation, in St. James Parish [west of New Orleans]. It was owned by White and Trufant and they raised sugarcane to make sugar.

"And then they parted an' my pa an' ma took us chil'ren to Gran' Prairie an' that's whar I growed up.

"The ol' folks used to say that the master was hard on slaves and had 'em whipped until the blood sometimes stained the groun'.

"My parents say they never was treated cruel like that 'cause they always wuz good, but my ont [aunt] said she was put in stocks 'cause she wouldn't give in.

"When we was little we never heard much talk 'cause chil'ren were never 'lowed to stay 'roun' grown folks when they wuz talkin', so I never heered much.

"They was a big pas'ly [parsley] bed on the place—and once I went to it an' dug up a whole lot an' laid down with my ear to the groun' a-lisnin' for a baby's cry. I staid there a long time but I never did hear anythin', an' then when they wanted to fin' out who did all that destruction, I up and owned that I wanted to fin' a baby. They knowed that they had tol' me that whar babies come from an' so they didn't whip me, but jes' laffed an' planted it all back again.

"I wuz raised right an' never did 'sociate with common niggers, like what they call the hoodoo kin'. In fac' I never heered of such things until I came to the city an' then I didn't until my husban' got pizened. A woman did it 'cause she wuz j'alous of me. He [was] all swolled up and got to coughin an' I sont [sic] to the drug store for some medicin'. When it didn't cure him arter eight days the drug-store man said nothin' would do him any good—that he wuz pizened by hoodoo.

"Now I believe in it, an' I never eat anythin' outside my house, not even in my own church."

"Your own church?"

"Yes'm those people are ev'rywhere, and Friday nights there is a supper, a fish fry to raise funds, but I never eat anythin'. I holp [sic] 'em to serve, ef they want me, but they never ask me.

"My ma useter say:

" 'Take keer, Marster' is better than 'O Lord, Marster.'

"Lor' a mussy [mercy]. Lor' a mussy!" cried Gracie. Looking across the street we saw the object of her supplication. A young negro woman was walking across the street in an abbreviated garb of short shorts.

"What are we a comin' to—when wimmen dress lik' that? It's the white folks set the style, an' niggers follow but more extreme.

"When I wus a growin' up, we wus taught jus' lak' white folks to keep our knees together an' our dresses down an' never to cross our legs. An' we wore long dresses too, but folks had raisin's then, an' the way they are carryin' on now, you don' know whut will happen.

"They don't talk niggerism any mo' either, an' they ain't got Mother Wit. They don' play lik' we did. We uster sing:

> Shoo chicken, shoo,
> You feed my chicken?
> Yes, mam!
> You brown my biscuit?
> Yes, mam!

"Then the leader would raise his hands an' say:

" 'Shoo chickens, shoo'—

"And every one would run jus' lak chickens do when they are bein' shooed. But I never hear things lak that now.

"Chil'ren mus' have money to go to picture shows. I never went to one in my life, 'cause they're ongodly [*sic*]. I'm told some churches have them with scenes from the Bible an' that's all right. My church aint got money enough for that.

"No'm, I ain' never been real sick in my life. If I look lak'

I goin' ta have headache I take Indian hand leaf an' steep it in vinegar, an' bin' [bind] it on my head. St. Jacob's quinine grows mos' ev'rywhere an' that's good for fevers.

"You see I was good to my parents an' minded them an' God's fulfilling His Comman'ment: 'That thy days may be long in the lan'.' That's the only Comman'ment that was given with a promis'. You know it says 'Honor thy Father an' thy Mother—that thy days may be long in the lan' which the Lord thy God giveth thee.'"

MRS. WEBB

Age: unknown
St. Philip Street, New Orleans, Louisiana
Interviewer: Michinard
August 17, 1940

[Mrs. Webb, otherwise unidentified, related the following story to the interviewer.]

The most cruel master in St. John Baptist [St. John the Baptist Parish is northwest of New Orleans on the "River Road"] during slavery time was a Mr. Valsin Mermillion.

One of his cruelties was to place a disobedient slave, standing, in a box, in which there were nails placed in such a manner that the poor creature was unable to move. He was powerless even to chase the flies, or sometimes ants crawling on some parts of his body.

A young slave who had been raised with the children of his master, had been very much spoiled and accustomed to all the good things on the plantation, at the death of his master was put on the block to be sold. Mr. Mermillion, who prided himself in having only handsome slaves, hearing of the fine physique of that young man, decided to have that slave at any price. He thereby bought him. The next day Mr. Mermillion, gave the order to put the young man to the plough. The man not accustomed to such rough work, refused to take the plough. The one giving the order said, "Were I in your place I would try it for you have no idea how mean is your Master." But the young man would not relent and refused to do such hard work. Mr. Mermillion hearing of this, went to the slave and told him, "I give you until tomorrow, if then you still refuse you will dig your grave."

The next day the boy had not yielded. He was then made to dig an immense hole in which they made him stand and bandaging his eyes he was shot, falling in the hole he had dug.

JULIA WOODRICH

Age: 89
415 Ocean Avenue, McDonoghville
Interviewer: McElwee
May 13, 1940

"Dey say, I was twelve years ol' when de battle was fought at Vicksburgh [*sic*], so you can figger up jes' how old I is. I was born at La Fouche Crossing. I don' know who my pa was. I think Ise de onliest one livin.

"Us first belong to Baugolis, a creole. He sho was a mean man. After he died us was auctioned off. My older brothers an' sisters was sold by deyselves but me. I was too young, I was sold along with my ma. We belonged to Guitlot. He was a Creole too—dats who we was sold to.

"My sisters, Mary an' Jane, an' Paul and Adam, was all sold an' sent off[. W]e never is knowed where dey went.

"Dey put dem up on a big stump an' de Boss would walk around with a big bullwhip on his shoulders, and see dat it was done right.

"My Ma had fifteen chillun, an' none of us had de same

pa—ever time she was sold she would git another man. Dey didn' sell de man dat she would be with.

"Dey didn't marry befo' de war; de Missus taken an alphabet, or some book, an' read somethin' out of it, and den put a broom down and dey jump over it—den dey was married. Sometimes dey would give dem a chicken supper.

"My Missus was good to us, but some of the other Massas was mean. Dey taken dem niggers on the levee an' whip dem with a bull whip. Dey use to holler 'Pray, Massa!' Dey would say, 'Dam you, pray yo'self!'

"Me, I wore little nightgowns, an' my brothers wore long shirts. We only had two suits a year. The missus wove the cloth. My job I done was to pick up de shuttle when it would fall and to water de chickens, but I done det every day. I slep in de house with my Missus on a pallet at de foot of de bed so's iffen she need anythin' I could brung it to her. . . .

"My maw had one boy by her Boss, that was my Missus' brother's chile. You see ever' time she was sold she had to take another man. Her had fifteen chilluns after she was sold de las' time; she was a good breeder. After the old folk die de young Massa and Missus divide every thing up, some taken land or money, but my Missus she taken the niggers[. S]he was a Cajun.

"Dey was not mean to me or my Ma either. I knows de only slapping Ise ever got, my Missus slapped me for stealing a biscuit. I jus' eased my hand threw [*sic*] her arm when she was making dem. We only had biscuit once a month.

"Ma an' my older sister would have to go across the bayou in the winter time to make grinding at the cane mills. Dey didn' get the pay, the Boss got it.

"Who? [U]s read! If you would have picked up a piece of paper they would have slapped your dam head off. I usto to [sic] deliver notes to the neighbor. Dey knew we couldn' read an' dey didn' want us to learn how, either. My Ma use to jump up and down and say: 'We gwine be free!' but iffen de Boss had of heard her she would have been put in de stocks—her hands, feet an' head. Dat would have been her punishment.

"De drivers would stand over de slaves with bull whips to see dat dey worked; de boss would come out on his big horse and give order. I seed de Missus tie up de women's coat-tails around dare waists for de driver to beat.

"But you know de poor white people did not have as much a show as us niggers. Dey treated dem awful.

"After us was sat [sic] free we stayed in a shack in de pasture. Our Messus told us she could not take care of us any longer. We lived off of berries and fish, crawfish and ever' thin' like that, for a long time after us was free. I got 'legion [religion] few years after I was free. I am the Mother of my church now.

"We usto have church in de ol' mill house. De Boss would stand in de door an' watch an' laugh at the womens shout—dey didn' do dat often, though.

"I 'member how my massa useto would come an' get my sister, make her take a bath an' comb her hair an' take her down in the quarter all night—den have de nerve to come aroun' de nex' day an' ax her how she feel. He useto wear a big straw hat[,] cottoneyed [sic] pants, an' red shoes. Dats de reason dare is so many mulatto nigger chillinns now."